WOMEN ON WATER

Women on
WATER

PADDLING THE ADIRONDACKS
AND CENTRAL NEW YORK

Ruth Dandrea · Kathy DeLong
Carol Moseman · Bonnie Sanderson

NORTH COUNTRY BOOKS, INC.
Utica, New York

Text Copyright © 2012 by Ruth Dandrea, Kathy DeLong,
Carol Moseman, and Bonnie Sanderson
Maps Copyright © 2012 by Maggie Henry
Photos Copyright © 2012 by Audrey Mihalko, unless otherwise noted
Design by Zach Steffen & Rob Igoe, Jr.

ISBN-10 1-59531-039-8
ISBN-13 978-1-59531-039-2

Library of Congress Cataloging-in-Publication Data

Women on water : paddling the Adirondacks and central New York / Ruth Dandrea ...
[et al.].
        p. cm.
    ISBN 978-1-59531-039-2 (alk. paper)
    1. Women canoeists--New York (State)--Adirondack Mountains. 2. Women canoeists--New York (State) 3. Canoes and canoeing--New York (State)--Adirondack Mountains--Guidebooks. 4. Canoes and canoeing--New York (State)--Guidebooks. 5. Adirondack Mountains (N.Y.)--Guidebooks. 6. New York (State)--Guidebooks. I. Dandrea, Ruth.
    GV777.57.W67 2012
    797.12209747--dc23
                                    2012008868

North Country Books, Inc.
220 Lafayette Street
Utica, New York 13502
www.northcountrybooks.com

WOW! Just a few old girls on boats.
We floats.
Seein' life from the water, paddlin' just as we oughter.
Wow! Just a few old girls on boats.

– WOW's "official" theme song

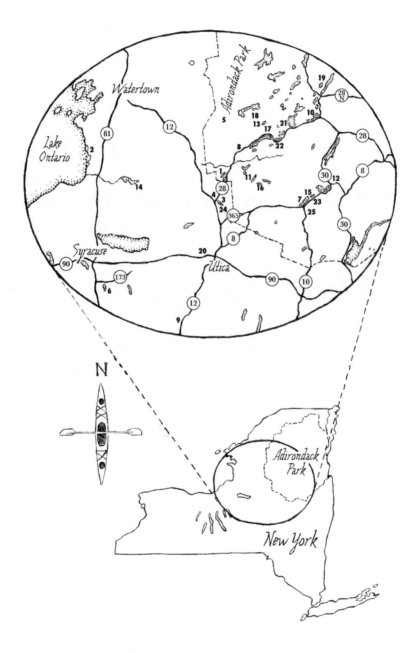

Contents

Audrey, Kathy, Ruth, Carol, and Bonnie on Little Long Lake

Foreword

Another guidebook? (ho-hum) A "how-to" for idiots? (yawn) Yet one more journal by over-the-hill women? (C'mon, they're a dime a dozen, and who cares?)

This little tome is really targeted and dedicated to our daughters, upon reaching "an age." We hope that by relating the experiences we have shared on the water, we will encourage them to join in our footsteps (wakes) and embrace the freedom of being a girl again, with kayak beneath, paddle in hand, and friends alongside.

Reflecting upon the many sights and stories we have enjoyed during our weekly journeys on the beautiful and varied waterways of Upstate New York, we have concluded that it's not about "how far or how fast" (as one fellow inquired as he raced past). After all, we are "just a few old girls on boats."

Introduction

This collection of stories reflects the joy and camaraderie shared over a period of several years by a group of upstate New York ladies commonly referred to as WOW – Women on Water. Our attempts to accurately describe the geographical locations, navigational data, and other "guidebook" references are sketchy at best. Rather, we intend to tell the stories of our journeys on the water as we have grown to be serious paddlers, explorers, and, most importantly, good friends.

The locations which we have chosen were selected from our many trips with several purposes in mind: to encompass a variety of water conditions which would appeal to beginning kayakers as well as the more experienced; to limit the overall commute to the Adirondacks and Central New York; and to share our favorite paddling experiences.

The sequence of entries is not chronological, but rather a pattern which best exemplifies the diversity of our days on the water. We have tried to order the chapters from early season (May–June) to summer (July–August) to fall (September–as late as we can go). This order reflects our experience on each waterway, and doesn't necessarily constitute a recommendation for a specific time of year.

As the book is not a comprehensive guidebook, a few things should be mentioned. First and foremost, safety issues can't be overemphasized. In order to really enjoy your experience in a kayak, you should be comfortable on and in the water. The best spots to get the knack of paddling are small, relatively shallow bodies of water that can be easily accessed from your car or carrier. (Swim instruction is offered at local YMCA's, YWCA's, and community colleges. Sporting goods dealers often hold classes in paddling kayaks and canoes.)

Weather conditions will influence the journey, so keep an eye on the local forecast, and choose your trip accordingly – i.e., stay away from a lake on a windy day; choose a secluded stream instead.

A U.S. Coast Guard-approved personal flotation device, or PFD, must be in each boat, and it is highly recommended that it be

Setting out on a brand new day

worn at all times. We suggest that someone in the group carry an extra paddle, first aid kit, bailer, and sponge. Each person should have a rope and whistle in her kayak.

The directions included in this book use Utica as a starting point. Each paddler must make adjustments according to her place of residence.

DeLorme's *New York Atlas and Gazetteer*, in combination with local road maps and internet mapping sites, provides accurate and extensive directions to launch sites. Although most New York State waterways are accessible to the public, many cross through private properties. This land is off-limits and trespassing is not allowed.

Paddling maps and GPS devices can be helpful in finding your way on and around the water, but don't rely on cell phone service, particularly in mountainous terrain. Let someone know where you are going and when you're planning to return.

We hope these collected memoirs provide inspiration and encouragement to those who will come after us, as we become "a few MORE old girls on boats."

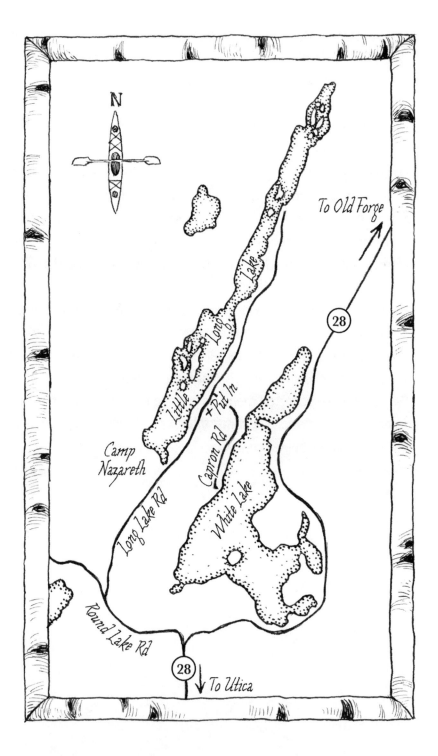

Little Long Lake

THE WAY THERE: Tucked just inside the southern seam of the Adirondack Park, Little Long Lake is reached by turning west from Route 28 on Round Lake Road and following the signs for Camp Nazareth. There is a public boat launch about halfway down the shoreline and a small parking area across the road.

REFLECTIONS ON THE WATER: Beckoned back to our boats by sunshine and an early spring, we head out on a pre-season paddle in mid-April. I am wearing a moisture-wicking layer, a wool turtleneck, a fleece hoodie, a winter-weight windbreaker, blue jeans, waterproof pants, fleece socks and water sandals, and fleece mittens. I am also wearing my life jacket, zipped up, knowing that a spill in these frigid waters, not to mention in this many clothes, would be disastrous.

Boarding our kayaks without walking in water is a tricky feat, but Bonnie, Kathy, and I manage it, and as soon as we are afloat on the still waters of Little Long Lake, it is as though we've returned home after a long absence. Everything just seems right. And good.

Even the multiple layers of clothes don't inhibit the paddling;

the stretch and pull of moving our boats through water is hypnotic and lulling. We soothe our way down the expanse of lake, listening. Beaver lodges litter the lakesides and floating bogs sport last year's pitcher plants, dried to red-brown distinction. In summer this place abounds with these plants and their cousins, the also carnivorous sundew. Below us the tangled vines of incipient pickerel weed wind like a million Medusa's heads. An occasional white-green sprout has matured enough to reveal its identifying arrowhead shape. It is these masses, I will learn from Audrey on a later paddle, that form the basis for the formation of the bogs.

We are lucky – the wind mostly misses us, pleated as we are into this long slice of protected water. There are no rustling leaves yet in these Adirondack foothills, no other people in boats; once we paddle past the batch of shoreline camps and nestle into the nooks and crannies to wait for wildlife, a turtle, a nesting goose to appear, we experience a deep, deep silence. We sit with it a long time.

Paddling back, Kathy spies a pair of loons. Somehow this magical bird has become a totem of a sort for WOW. I don't know a paddler who won't stop, sitting still, for as long as it takes, to watch a loon. Today it surprises me to realize that the closer our kayaks drift to the pair, the harder they become to see, merging as they do with the dappled water. They stay. And so do we.

When we finally part, it is as fellow paddlers. The birds swim just beyond us, never diving, never in a hurry, as if we are simply another breed of waterfowl sharing their lovely lake. It is the greatest of compliments. Ted Andrews, in his book *Animal Speaks*, identifies the loon as symbol of the "re-awakening of old hopes, wishes and dreams." If he is right, the summertime dreams of women on water are burgeoning forth in the new spring growth.

Before we return to the put-in and disembark, a dozen hawks

Cold paddling on thick water

circle us high in the sky. A last connection.

The sublimity of the experience dissipates as we carry our boats to the cars, fasten straps with numbed fingers, feel the chill that's settled in our bones. Bonnie turns her ignition to check the temperature. Forty-five degrees. "I'm so glad we did this," she says. So is Kathy. So am I.

DIVERSIONS: There aren't any – which is the best reason to go.

WHAT YOU SHOULD CONSIDER: Prior to May 1, New York State law demands that paddlers wear, not carry, their life preservers. Even in the cold, you need to hydrate; bring a water bottle.

IS IT WORTH THE TRIP? First forays always are.

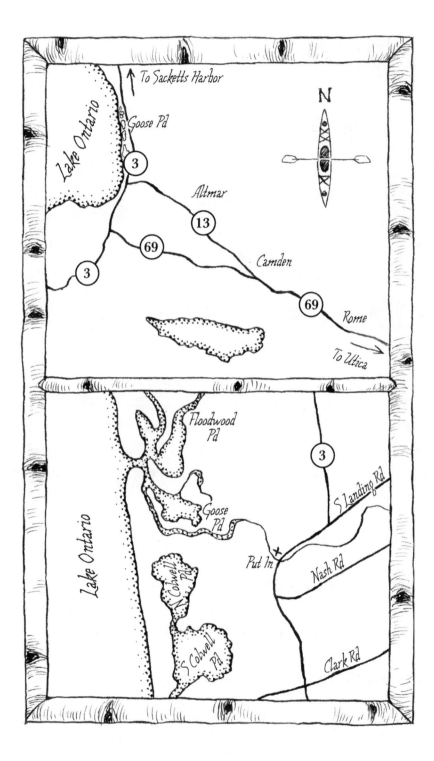

Goose Pond, Lake Ontario

My left side is covered in mud, heel to hip, from a slight slip of the foot while dragging my kayak down the shallow bank to the water. I am not alone. Jude tries a different route and she lands on her butt. Carol loses her footing and is wearing a coat of slick black goo.

THE WAY THERE: Follow Route 49 from Utica to Rome, then Route 69 to Camden, and Route 13 to Pulaski. Head into town and take Route 5. Turn right on Route 3 (north) until you see a parking area to the left on the north side of South Sandy Creek (about 12 miles). There are some interpretive signs, a boat launch, a bathroom (yea!), and a trail.

REFLECTIONS ON THE WATER: Jean has been wanting us to come here, and today, a sunny, warm, late-spring day, seems like the perfect time to do so. We had some serious rain last week, so the creek is high and the banks, we discover, are covered with a slick, silty mud. We should have guessed, as the ground sloshes between our toes and our sandals as we carry our kayaks toward the shore. Jude and Bonnie use the boat launch; Jean, Carol,

Ruth, and I think the bank is the better bet. Neither is easy, and half of us meet the mud. Dirtied but undaunted, we climb in our boats and head downstream, the current swift but flat. A small motorboat with two fishermen on its way upstream crosses our paths. We have no idea what adventures are in store.

The paddle is easy for about fifteen minutes. We are exploring the shoreline, catching up on news: Jude's daughter is pregnant; Carol's transferred to San Francisco; Bonnie and I are planning a trip to Italy.

As we look ahead, we see a tangle of downed trees, so we back-paddle to the side of the stream to assess the situation. Because parts of the river are blocked, the flow is now narrow and fast. There seems to be an area to the left to enter the tangle, then a small dam of sticks between two logs straight ahead of that. Or, we could enter the tangle and make a quick right turn, head toward the right bank, then make a quick left to clear the thicket of debris. Jean first. She opts for the small dam, gets stuck, and begins to work herself through as she pulls broken branches out one by one. Jude takes the quick right and gets pushed aside into the snarl, backs up, re-aims her kayak, paddles furiously, and shoots out. Jean is still on the dam. I am next and attempt to follow Jude, but my kayak is long and sits deeper in the water than the others, and I get pushed into the logjam. As I struggle to move forward, the current keeps tipping my kayak against the logs. I try to push against them with my paddle, scenes from *Deliverance* running through my head. Ruth positions herself to offer me an assist with her paddle, I grab it, she pulls, and suddenly I am within arm's reach of a solid overhead branch. Jean is just breaking through the dam. With all my might, I pull myself up, shift my hips to swing the kayak facing downstream, and let go. The dam stops me too, but removal of a few more sticks frees me and will allow Ruth and Carol easy passage if they can aim their kayaks to the newly opened channel. Bonnie somehow escapes my notice and follows Jude without too much difficulty.

All of us through, we enjoy our leisurely float toward Lake Ontario. The grass is high on both sides; there are dead tree stumps, a great blue heron, families of ducks.

After a while we reach Goose Pond, paddle across, and see an inlet to Lake Ontario. The wind out here is incredibly strong! Waves are crashing into the shore. We force ourselves across the inlet. Boats ashore, we grab our lunches, walk along the beach, and sit on a log amongst the gulls. We are not alone. There is a couple across the inlet, but we see no evidence of how they happened to get there. It is very windy even on the lee side of the inlet, and our food is gritty with the airborne sand.

After our beachcombing break, we cross the choppy cove to explore Floodwood Pond. We find ourselves spreading apart across the water, examining the differences in lily pads, identifying flowers, watching birds overhead, and enjoying the breeze off the lake in this sheltered environment. I surmise that we are postponing the paddle back upstream. Eventually, we spontaneously gather together to begin our return trip and face that logjam from the other direction.

Along the way we meet a couple in a canoe who have entered Goose Pond from the Colwell Ponds, a smarter approach of which we were unaware.

As we close in on our destination, the current picks up and we start to look for an egress that we can use instead of having to make our way through the labyrinth ahead. There is a clearing with a bench that offers possibilities, so we paddle over. The bank is vertical, and about shoulder high. Ruth reaches for the

Sometimes you have to be wiling to stick your neck out

streambed with her paddle. Too deep. Too dangerous. We press on. As we approach the hazard, Carol notices that there may be a pass to the left of the tangle but to the right of a rock with a smaller web of branches. We will have to back up and get a good head of steam going into the current so we can power past the swirling water. Carol first, then Bonnie. One by one until all of us have safely navigated through the obstruction.

Back at the put-in, we all head for the boat launch. Muscles burning, we heave our tired bodies from the cockpits and gingerly slip our sandals back into the mud, grab the ropes on the front of our kayaks and carefully make our way to solid footing. With assists from each other, we pull our kayaks up the ramp through the muck and load them on our cars.

We are a bedraggled bunch with mud to our ankles, on our clothes, and in our hair, but none of us are in a hurry to head home, so we decide to take the trail. It leads to a great seagrass prairie with an elevated platform from which to view it. There, the sun warms our tired muscles and we look back with satisfaction on a great adventure. Life is good, the whole summer is ahead of us, and...we passed an ice cream stand in Pulaski.

DIVERSIONS: There is a fish hatchery in Altmar where, at the right time of year, they milk salmon, and fishing launches are plentiful in the area. History buffs may visit the Sackets Harbor Battlefield (War of 1812) and burial site of Zebulon Pike.

CONSIDERATIONS: Distance could be an issue; the drive was a good two hours for us. This wasn't a trip for a first-time paddler, as it was a difficult paddle and dangerous at times. I thought for an instant that I should have brought an extra paddle. We did not go back, so I don't know what the current condition of the river is, but since this is an important fishing area, it's hopefully been cleaned up by now.

IS IT WORTH THE TRIP? Wouldn't have missed it for the challenge.

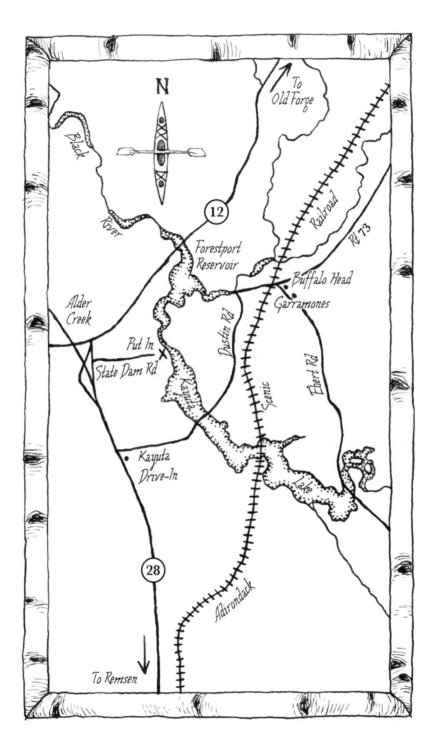

Kayuta Lake

THE WAY THERE: The lake is easy to reach. Travel north on Route 12 past Remsen. At Alder Creek, bear right onto Route 28 as if you are heading to Old Forge. Turn right almost immediately onto State Dam Road and follow the road to the end. Parking is available and you may launch your kayak right above the dam. There are no bathroom facilities.

REFLECTIONS ON THE WATER: A mere twenty miles from Utica, Kayuta Lake is a great place for a novice kayaker. The lake is divided into three sections and can be accessed from either the lower or upper part.

Our group has paddled the lake numerous times, and several of us have camps here. This morning we put in at the dam and head up the lake following the shoreline. The water is dark from the tannic acid of the Black River which flows into the upper section. It looks like black velvet in the early morning sunshine. We pass numerous camps and investigate two inlets off to the right. In July, the lake abounds with bottled gentian and the banks are alive with purple blooms. Ducks are plentiful, as are Canada geese. A stop at the islands is a must. There is a large sandbar and a swim is mandatory. During the week, this spot is relatively quiet. On the weekends, though, the islands are a mass of humanity with boats, jet skis, and party barges. Beware! Wakes can be a problem for a kayaker.

We travel under the Dustin Road Bridge and see the message chalked on the I-beam about a Kayuta Lake Improvement Association boat parade. As we paddle past camps large and small, we notice that all the residents have string, rope, or chicken wire across their beaches put there to serve as geese deterrents. As on many Adirondack lakes, the Canada geese have become an increasing problem; I count thirty on one lawn. Considering that one goose can produce a pound of droppings per day, residents are not all that happy that the geese have chosen Kayuta Lake as their home.

Now in the middle section of the lake, we paddle towards the railroad trestle that separates the middle and end portions. During the summer, the Adirondack Scenic Railroad conducts trips from Utica to Thendara, and today we hear a whistle in the distance. As the train approaches, we halt our paddle to wave at the passengers, who snap photographs of our colorful kayaks.

As we head into the upper section of the lake, we bear right into Baker Brook inlet, a lily pond filled with flowers, herons, and ducks. The pond can be quite shallow in places, and some of us have to backtrack several times to find the deeper sections. Getting stuck in the muck is worth the headache because the inlet narrows to a small stream. Older camps loom above us on one side as we approach several beaver dams. Some of us are more proficient than others in finding our way across the obstacles, but by pulling and pushing, we are all successful. A kingfisher announces our presence and we see raccoon tracks in the mud. The inlet ends at a rocky waterfall where we turn around and shoot the rapids downstream.

Once out on the lake, we head to Ebert's Bridge, the demarcation of Kayuta Lake and the Black River. Some of the women have planned ahead and have a car waiting at this end of the lake. The rest of us paddle back and make one more side trip up an inlet near the trestle. Unfortunately, the area is filling in with sand and we cannot make much progress. The towering pines, the silence, and the numerous turtles sunning themselves on the logs mitigate our frustration.

DIVERSIONS: You can put in below Kayuta Lake dam and float downstream into Forestport Reservoir, a nice excursion in the fall. An ice cream cone at Kayuta Drive In is well worth it. You may also travel to Forestport to the Buffalo Head Restaurant or Garramone's Restaurant for dinner.

CONSIDERATIONS: If you circumnavigate the lake, you will probably be in your kayak for at least four hours. Wind can be a factor in the afternoon, but hugging the shoreline usually solves the problem. Boat traffic is a definite disturbance on the weekends.

IS IT WORTH THE TRIP? Yes, especially since you can vary the trip and its length by paddling the sections of the lake on different days.

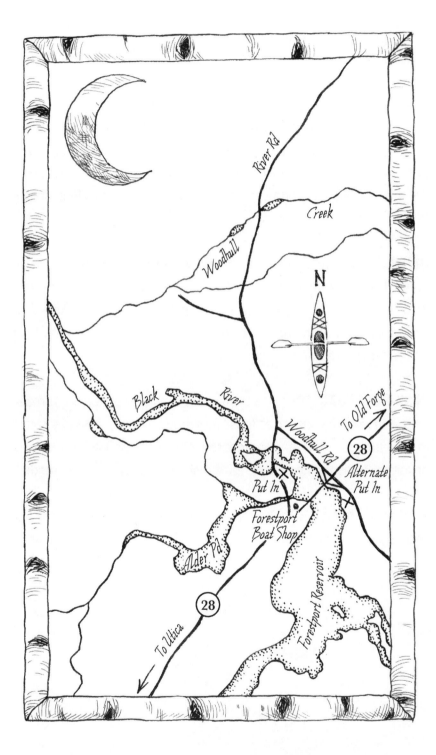

Moonlight Paddle, Forestport Reservoir

A magical evening...an apt description for this event...the unexpected kayak reunion of friends who haven't paddled together (or seen each other) since last summer...a few bottles of wine, complete with Kathy's elegant plastic goblets...and...the full moon casting her light over the water's gently rippling surface.

THE WAY THERE: Take Route 12/28 north of Utica and stay on Route 28 when it branches off to the right at Alder Creek. Follow this to Forestport and exit. Turn left at the Forestport Boat Company and park just above the dam.

REFLECTIONS ON THE WATER: Although this paddle – Forestport Reservoir under a full moon – is scheduled to "kick off" the season, thunderstorms blow in and out of the area all day long, and we decide to cancel the event at the last minute. Too late...a few of the ladies are already enroute and have no intention of letting a few storm clouds spoil the evening! As the locals say, "If you don't like the weather, wait ten minutes and it will change to something you *might* like!"

We launch our boats above the dam and head upriver, past the little hamlet where families are bustling about their evening activities along the shoreline. No hurry for us, however, as we take our leisurely time dipping the paddles in the dark, chilly water and keep a running commentary from boat to boat of all the "happenings" that have transpired since we were last together.

We cross the reservoir and call out to a couple of fishermen who are as happy as we are to be back on the water after the long cold winter. They are fishing from kayaks, which impresses us. Maybe there's hope for a motorless world!

We paddle to the dam at Kayuta Lake and turn around to find Kathy gaining on us...she had a late start, but brings wine, and with Heidi's chocolate, a party is about to begin. Six of us hold onto each other's boat as the wine is poured and the chocolate passed...we're a veritable raft of chatting WOW girls, sharing our stories once again. The snowbirds tell of their winter in the sun, and those of us who brave (indeed, relish) the snows of the north country relate our tales. As the wine is poured across the little fleet, again and yet again, the stories continue until our memories (faulty, at best) begin wavering.

Finally, we are still and listen to the night...now the magic of moonlight on the water begins.

The sky darkens and the moon rises higher, guiding us through the weeds and lily pads into a series of rapids in Woodhull Creek. We take turns trying to steer a path through the rocks and the current, without much success...first one gets hung up on a rock, then another gets tossed right around while attempting a rescue. We power our way through the rushing water, only to have the current grab our boats and send them back down the stream. Heidi and Eileen are undaunted...the combination of tenacity and chocolate push their kayaks beyond the point where others fail to go.

The rest of us submit to the inevitable and allow the force of the water to push us slowly back to the reservoir, where we wait for the powerful duo to return with their tales of derring-do.

Suddenly a loud slap against the water tells us that we are intruding into Mr. Beaver's personal space. It is too dark to see him, but another slap gives a clue to his whereabouts, and we're aware there are fellow creatures of the night as we slowly make our way back to the cars with the moon behind us and Venus shining high in the western sky.

We're so glad that we ignored the weather reports tonight.

DIVERSIONS: There is more paddling available on the feeder canal, Kayuta Lake, or another pond across the road from our launch site. The rocks below the Forestport Dam are great for a picnic. The Kayuta Drive In, Garramone's, or the Buffalo Head are nearby restaurants, where you can get ice cream, a good meal, or a few drinks at reasonable prices.

CONSIDERATIONS: Paddling in the dark presents unique challenges; be prepared to run into rocks and other unseen obstructions. Our boats are quite sturdy, so we don't worry much about puncturing them, but others (including those made of Kevlar) might not fare as well. We purposely choose an area with which we are familiar, as the dangers of exploring the unknown with only headlamps or flashlights are formidable. Lifejackets are mandatory. As any venture in the wilderness would warrant, awareness of the entire party and a frequent accounting of members is important. (And be sure to go easy on the wine!)

IS IT WORTH THE TRIP? A moonlight paddle is truly magical, and we would highly recommend it, particularly with dear friends or family.

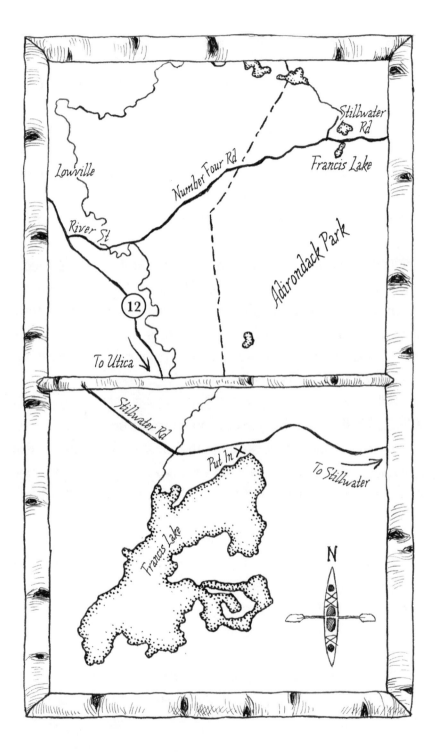

Francis Lake

THE WAY THERE: Head north on Route 12. Number Four Road will be on your right just as you're entering Lowville. Follow it to a right onto Stillwater Road. Francis Lake will also be on the right. There is a clearly marked put-in with parking for just a car or two, but there is lots of parking along the edges of the very-much less-traveled road that brings you there. The put-in can also be reached via Eagle Bay on Big Moose Road, but there is a long unpaved stretch to traverse from that direction. (Still, it might be worth the trek, since from Eagle Bay it is only a quick jaunt to the Northern Lights Creamery in Inlet and their delectable gelato!)

REFLECTIONS ON THE WATER: Francis Lake offers the quintessential Adirondack quiet-water paddling experience. We are lured to it en masse. On this sticky-hot Thursday morning, fifteen women slide into their boats. We wind our way from the dock, pulling silently away. Without consultation, the cavalcade of colorful boats drifts toward the westernmost shore, passes the promontory where some campers are fishing, and slips into the still waters of an enclosed bay lush with water lilies, pitcher plants, candle flowers, and some sweet yellow bloom none of us can identify. The density of the undergrowth creates little rivers in which to lose oneself, to separate from other paddlers, then rejoin them around the next bend. It is beautiful, and we are glad to be back. Back together, back to summer, back to the water.

This is not our first WOW paddle of the year, but it is the first so widely attended. Paddlers sidle their boats in pairs to catch up on the long winter's doings, then do-si-do to the next conversant. I head out with Annie, who, though she lives a mere mile from me, I have not seen once since last summer. We talk of kids and work, the thrill of being back in our boats, the exquisite beauty of the world around us. I do not know what the others talk about, because we have stretched ourselves into a long chain, a colorful necklace along the southern shore of the lake, whose bounty seems limitless, timeless, and ageless.

It is that usual urging – hunger – that reconfigures the group. Sue, Jude, and I are ready for lunch. We stream ahead, searching for a good mooring. Audrey, who has been here before, tells us that when she and Carol kayaked here a few weeks earlier, they ate on the promontory where we'd seen the boys fishing. "It was the best place," she reminisces. "Beautiful and an easy in and out." We question her more, anxious for the morsels we've tucked in our wet bags. "I don't know," she says, wryly. "After we found the best place to eat, we didn't look for the second best place."

We have heard the story of what they did do, though. Because Carol is in New Mexico this week acting in another of her many roles – Grandma to baby Levin – and because she didn't want to miss this little pearl of a paddle, she and Audrey previewed it before our group trip. And Carol, swatting at a deer fly, lost her glasses. At the bottom of the lake. So Audrey, our former gym teacher; Audrey, our faithful photographer; Audrey, our warehouse of plant knowledge; Audrey, who never removes her kayak from its rack atop her car all summer long even if she's not planning a trek (who knows, she tells us, you might pass a pond and just feel the need to put in); Audrey, who dragged each of us over our first beaver dam; Audrey, the only one of us to keep track of her mileage (five hundred last summer); Audrey decided there was no point in sending a blind woman searching the muck for her own glasses and said, "Oh, I'll do it." Carol breathed a huge "whew," and Audrey, swimsuit-less that afternoon, stripped and dove and found the glasses for Carol. Then continued the paddle, topless. Life jackets can save your life in more ways than one!

The second best place for lunch, Jude and I decide, is the downed tree trunk jutting into the water in a small cove not too far from the put-in. She paddles herself backward into the vegetation, enough to get a bit stuck; I slide alongside; we cross our paddles over each other's boats to maintain the position, and pull out our sandwiches, vegetables, and fruit. This being an early expedition, we are not quite as well-provisioned as we like to be – it takes awhile to get back into the routine of remembering what to pack. Annie, who pulls in next, has forgotten her water bottle; we all offer her a sip, and I fortify her with some watermelon until Bonnie arrives and offers her extra water bottle. Audrey has forgotten her lunch, but Jude's got an extra meat pie from Karam's – a favorite delicacy. We share sliced peppers, carrots, and cherries. Everyone offers a sample.

Because we were so stretched out on the lake, some of us are finished eating when others arrive. We have some additions to our usuals this week. Kathy's sister Gail has joined us for the first time, so her stories are especially welcomed. Celia, whom we first met on the Kunjamuk a couple summers ago, is a little bit of a local legend among us. The trek up the Kunjamuk to Elm Lake was the longest and most strenuous we'd done to date. And there was Celia, who'd never before paddled a boat, and she trudged along with us, the whole way! What can't women do?

The after-paddle swim is mandatory. Those who've gone ahead have beached their boats and are wading off a small sandy shore. Beyond it Bonnie identifies one of the many eskers, glacier-made ridges, that surround and enclose this lake. She abandons her boat, dives, and swims for it. Aloft, she calls for the rest of us to join her. "Are you going?" Annie asks me. "Bonnie is my former boss," I tell her, "When she says swim to the rock, I swim to the rock." Many of us do. It is a slippery climb up, but there are directions to the footholds, and Gail is now on top, offering each new arrival a helping hand. Jude dubs Bonnie "Esker Williams."

Our after-swim includes an exploration of the shoreline towards the small falls and smaller bridge. We can hear the tumbling waters, but not see them.

The lake is beautiful, but it won't be an all-day paddle today. Since the temperatures are in the nineties and the sun is relentless, we don't mind. Paddlers reach the dock for take-out in small groups. The campers have returned from the promontory and are assembled in the woods. One counselor comes down to the dock to steady Gail's boat as she disembarks. Kiddingly, I tease him, "You might not want to do that. There are fifteen of us." But he does do it. For every WOW paddler who needs his help. Moreover, he directs the younger boys under his supervision to carry our boats out for us. And they do. All fifteen boats carried to our cars and trucks, lifted to our roof racks, slid inside the truck beds. We offer to tip these fine young gentlemen from Beaver Camp, but they decline. Chivalry in their neck of the woods, they assure us, is an art alive and flourishing.

Not loading our own boats is a rare treat; the ice cream we stop to eat at Mercer's Dairy, just north of Boonville on Route 12, a familiar, but no less satisfying one.

A Francis Lake paddle on a hot July day? Afloat on a pristine lake, you're surrounded by towering pines and alone with the wildflowers and birdsong. As the narrator from Jonathan Safran Foer's novel, *Extremely Loud and Incredibly Close*, might say, "If you looked up summer in the dictionary, this would be its definition."

DIVERSIONS: Nearby there is only woods. Further down the road is the Stillwater Reservoir with its boat trips to The Norridgewock Lodge. Further back is Lowville.

CONSIDERATIONS: Don't let it keep you from swimming, but our first sightings from the dock were of two too-long leeches undulating their way around the supports. We opted not to wade in, but to board our boats from the dock, even though it's a bit more challenging. "There are leeches in every lake we paddle," Bonnie assures us. Usually, however, we do not see them. Outside of that scene in the movie *Stand By Me*, I have never seen them. To feel them, I'm not inclined. "All you have to do," someone else offers, "is put salt on them." I will bet someone has already slid a saltshaker into her wet bag for our next expedition.

Also, the last gas is in Lowville. (And, in case you ever need one, as Jude did after losing hers at an early morning fill-up further south, the hardware store in Boonville carries replacement gas caps.)

IS IT WORTH THE TRIP? Indubitably. This is what quiet water paddling is all about.

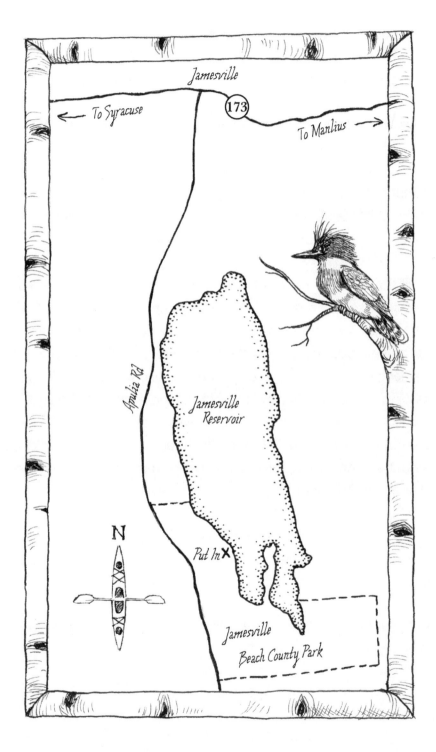

Jamesville

To Syracuse ←

173

To Manlius →

Apulia Rd

Jamesville
Reservoir

N

Put In ✗

Jamesville
Beach County Park

6 Jamesville Reservoir

"I see what they mean about the wind."

THE WAY THERE: From Route 5 or Route 173 east from Syracuse or west from Manlius, take Apulia Road south 1.9 miles from Jamesville. Jamesville County Park is on the left. There is an entry fee that varies by day, hour, and age.

REFLECTIONS ON THE WATER: As I leave the house this morning, I tell my husband I have an uneasy feeling about today's paddle. When he asks why, I can only answer, "I don't know. Probably just the first time with my new carrier." (Thule J racks)

"Relax," he says. "Have fun." He's always encouraging me to hit the road with my friends.

We are only four. Carol, Audrey, and I are meeting at Ruth's house for a rare trip west. Everyone we speak to is declining. I have to admit, we are Adirondack snobs; the mountains and lakes are so beautiful, fragrant, and comfortable. Today, we are going to Syracuse, for goodness sake, to kayak. What are we thinking?

We head west, through Rome, Oneida, Chittenango, Manlius. We pull into the park, read the sign; I ask for a two dollar senior pass and am told that it's free for me until noon. We park our cars and head for the bathroom. I swear, this is the cleanest public toilet I have ever used. Score a point for Jamesville Reservoir.

As we walk back to our cars, we see another with a kayak on top. It's Sue, and she's almost ready to leave. We are all glad to see her. She says she was looking to buy a house on this lake but thinks she will buy a new kayak instead. We unload our boats, carry them down to the shore and lower ourselves in. "I see what they mean about the wind!" I exclaim.

Jamesville Reservoir is dammed on the north end and it is fed by Butternut Creek on the south. Jamesville County Park is very near the inlet of the creek. The wind is coming from the north, creating rollers as we paddle from the shore, so we decide to seek the shelter of the creek. Carol informs us that the guide we are using says Butternut Creek will be obvious. Not to us. We paddle right by (we later discover) in favor of what appears to be

Portaging the shallows

a wider cut. As we cross the lake we keep to the right, passing small turtles sunning on logs. A heron takes off into the wind and appears to hover before he gets up a head of steam and moves on. We can see that this is not the creek. Back we go to check out the marsh we passed. This is the creek. Audrey leads, camera in her lap as she makes the first turn. By the time her camera is to her eye she has missed the belted kingfisher.

As we make the next turn, I look up. There, in a tree, three and a half feet above me, is wrack, a cluster of debris left by high spring runoff. It appears the water is still much higher than summer level as we cross branches and logs. And the current is strong, so if we stop paddling, we will quickly lose ground.

We make a couple more turns, passing sycamores, cress, and forget-me-nots, all while Audrey is identifying birds from their calls. She spots a sandbar and I am grateful that she suggests lunch, even though it is only eleven thirty.

While we are eating, a woman approaches with a small curly-haired dog and we talk about the trails. She has been walking for forty-five minutes and says that unleashed dogs are accepted on this part of the trail. Not long after, another woman, this time with two chocolate labs, comes along. Marley, the larger of the two, knocks Ruth's open water bottle over, then the two pups cavort in the water for a time. After Marley and Gracie leave with their owner, three of us lament over being dogless, all the while realizing how much more complicated our lives would be if we still had animals.

We leisurely finish our lunches. Audrey, Ruth, and Carol decide to continue upstream. The creek is maybe six feet wide and six inches deep. There is a current, and I can see that this is a futile exercise. I am traveling alone and am anxious and apprehensive about loading my kayak on the J racks by myself. As it is, Sue

"Sitting on the dock of the ..."

decides to come back with me, leaving the others to explore the lake proper. Despite my resistance, she helps me. My crossbars are round and I can't tighten the racks enough to keep them from shifting as I push my kayak up from the back of the car. We both are too short to lift it over the hook of the J even when I use the footstool. We eventually get it up, and I am so grateful for the help. I can see I will have to modify the system but am relieved to realize that once my kayak is strapped down, it is incredibly secure.

Heading home, I consider my day. The paddle was pleasant, if short. I ponder solutions to the rack system and mentally design the perfect one. I will continue being apprehensive until I determine how to load my boat by myself.

DIVERSIONS: The Jamesville Park hosts a triathlon and a hot air balloon festival. There are trails to hike, and Chittenango Falls is a worthwhile side trip. Syracuse is nearby, with all it has to offer.

"On the road again"

CONSIDERATIONS: The wind can be treacherous.

IS IT WORTH THE TRIP? Definitely! You don't have to worry about gas or provisions. Access is easy and it is only four miles from Syracuse.

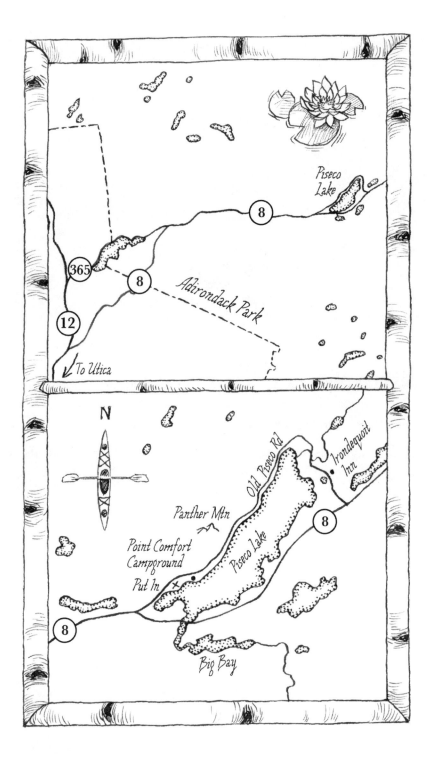

Big Bay, Piseco Lake

THE WAY THERE: Piseco Lake is located fifty-four miles north of Utica. Take Route 12 north, exit at Route 365 and head east. Route 365 will end at Route 8. Turn left and travel to Piseco. Turn left on Old Piseco Lake Road and drive to Point Comfort State Park. You may launch your boat from the site after paying a fee. Senior citizens are free. Bathrooms are available.

REFLECTIONS ON THE WATER: It is another sunny day, and all twelve of us are excited for a new paddle. The red, blue, yellow, orange, and green kayaks are launched, and we head directly across the lake from the state park. A large rock with a smiling green frog painted on the side indicates our turn into Piseco Lake outlet.

Kayaking under the Route 8 overpass is not a problem, but we notice large rocks both above and below the surface of the water immediately after the bridge. Sue owns a beautiful Kevlar kayak and has to be extra cautious not to scrape the bottom. We paddle counterclockwise around the rocks and enter Big Bay.

Big Bay is secluded, scenic, and special. Today it is calm. Puffy cumulus clouds are reflected in the water as we paddle by vast expanses of pines. An occasional cardinal plant can be seen – an

A gaggle of girls

absolutely brilliant red against green moss. There are numerous rock outcroppings and acres of water lilies. We tie up at a large boulder and clamber out to enjoy the summer day. Lunches are shared, stories are told and retold, and we discuss future days on the water. A small plane passes overhead, and we are sure the pilot must be amazed to see twelve women in their fifties, sixties, and seventies sitting on a rock enjoying the view.

On the return trip, we pass pickerel weed in bloom and skirt our way around dead tree trunks. A wood duck house is tacked onto one of the trees and a family of mallards lurks in the under-growth. A small stream is worth investigating, and Audrey leads the way over a beaver dam.

As we return to Piseco Lake, we take a side trip under a low wooden foot bridge and more than one of us sings "Low bridge, ev'rybody down." Sailboats and motorboats announce our arrival. We all agree that a return paddle in the fall is essential.

DIVERSIONS: A trip to Piseco Lake should also include hiking Panther Mountain. The trailhead is on the opposite side of the road from the campground. The trail leads to a seven-hundred-foot cliff, aptly named Echo Cliffs. The forty-five minute hike up the mountain is well worth the effort. Views of Piseco Lake and the surrounding Adirondack Mountains are terrific. Do not hesitate to shout, shout, shout, and hear the resounding echo, echo, echo!

The Piseco Lake Triathlon takes place annually in July. You may enter individually or as a team – or you might just watch the athletes swim a half mile, bike eleven and one-half miles, and run three miles. The race begins on the shore of the historic Irondequoit Inn (established in 1892).

Should you have a pilot's license, you can fly into Piseco Lake Airport, a small airport that caters to summer tourists and those who want to savor the fresh mountain air and enjoy the fishing.

CONSIDERATIONS: As with any large body of water, wind is a factor. For the novice kayaker, choose a day when the forecast is for calm breezes.

IS IT WORTH THE TRIP? Yes. The view of the Adirondack Mountains and Big Bay make you glad you have chosen to kayak in this natural setting. A fall trip will overwhelm you with the colors.

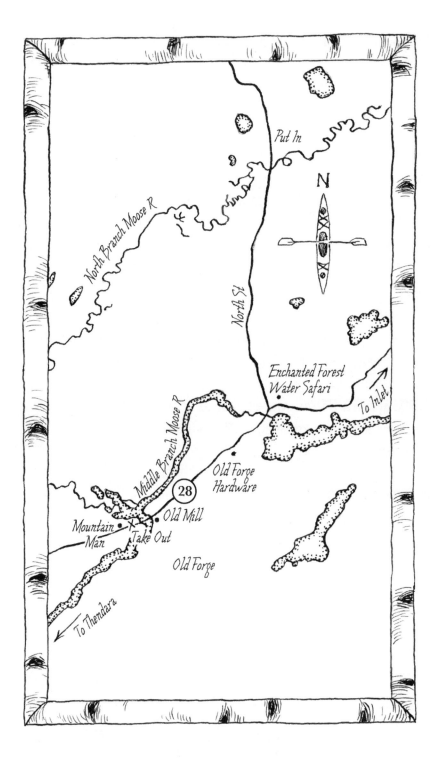

Moose River

THE WAY THERE: From Route 28, we put in at North Road in Old Forge, across from the Pied Piper, before the Enchanted Forest.

REFLECTIONS ON THE WATER: Wrapped in the sinuous arms of the Moose River, our column of colorful kayaks winds its way, leisurely and long. It is just the water, the green grasses on the banks, with the woods beyond, the sandy beaches, the sensuous smell of cedar, and us. Every so often the dark red of a single cardinal flower shouts to us from the shoreline like an exclamation point on a perfect day. Each time the river bends, the view is more beautiful than the last.

This is a different kind of paddle, one with a destination. Instead of rambling we move ever forward, like the river itself. Time passes slowly in a small boat on flowing water, but pass it does, so every detail must be noticed, recognized. Stacey, the science teacher among us, spots the tiny carnivorous sundew along the bank, its small green face open to passing insect food. We are also introduced to a bizarre, frondy form of moss called liverwort. We are exalted by small things, humbled by the largesse of open sky and ancient waters.

And this chair is just right!

Other people share the river, and it seems right to greet fellow paddlers and those we pass picnicking on the banks. The tradition of the gathering place makes us one.

This trip marks a milestone for our group. For it is on the ride north from breakfast that Bonnie, a former music teacher, composes our theme song. She bubbles out its words and melody, and before long the river echoes our refrain:

WOW! Just a few old girls on boats.
We floats.
Seein' life from the water, paddlin' just as we oughter.
WOW! Just a few old girls on boats.

It suits us, and we know it. We are happy to be here, happy to be together, happy to still learn, to try, to grow, to appreciate, to respect our world. As we grow together, we join the intricate web of water, air, and earth which carries and nurtures us. WOW!

The trip is memorable for many reasons. This section of the Moose River provides us with our first (and only) portage. Our takeout place, the bridge spanning Route 28 from the Mountainman Outdoor Supply Company to the Old Mill Restaurant, is a familiar spot to all travelers entering the mountains via Thendara and Old Forge. The water below almost always boasts a brace of paddlers. Many's the time we've watched from car windows, envying those afloat on the river beneath us. Today we are those kayakers. Faces in the windows of passing cars look down to us, wish they were where we are, want to trade places with us. But we do not want to trade places with anybody. We do not want to leave this river. We float under the bridge, attempt a take out, find it too rocky, and paddle upstream to Mountainman Outdoor Supply Company, where the proprietors graciously allow us to take out on their dock. Two of us wait with the boats while the others retrieve our cars. By now we are old hands at loading and tying the kayaks. As we trudge up the hillside carrying boat after boat, one young man who works at the store congratulates us. "It's really good," he compliments, "that women like you are still doing this."

"Women like us?" we wonder.

Why, we're "WOW! Just a few old girls on boats."

DIVERSIONS: The village of Old Forge can occupy any summer's afternoon even without a Moose River paddle. An abundance of craft stores, eating establishments, parks, and beaches offer something for of everyone. The must-see, must-stop place is, of course, the Old Forge Hardware store. Learn about the history of the store and what's in it (what's not?). Visit the Water Safari or View (the Old Forge arts center). Stay at the Nick's Lake campground or the Old Forge Camping Resort. Take the scenic chair lift ride at McCauley Mountain, and look for the deer and maybe bear on South Shore Road. Hike Bald or Rocky Mountains. We are most assuredly quiet water paddlers, but if you hearken to a wilder call, other areas of the Moose River will provide thrills for any white-water seeker.

CONSIDERATIONS: Even the wildly winding branch of this river that we slowly trek on a leisurely summer's day unleashes a minor cascade about two miles above the take-out. The carry looks longer than it actually is. We walk it first without boats to judge the arduousness of the journey, and though it makes for more footsteps, at least we aren't wandering into woods on a narrow path with a boat in each hand wondering how much far-ther we have to go. We take our time. We help each other. We prefer more light trips to fewer heavy ones. We are glad to be

Warnings on the water

beyond the riffles, but they are lovely to look at and give us our only taste of thrill-ride excitement as we paddle our boats upstream a bit to enjoy the downward thrust of the water. Plus we get to meet fascinating people who've kayaked upstream just to run these same rapids we plod boat-laden to avoid. So they are sometimes navigable, if that is your bent. (Though a sign before the rapids warns that if you are paddling a rented boat, you must portage.)

IS IT WORTH THE TRIP? Definitely; however, consideration must be taken regarding water levels. Deciding to include this wonderful journey again in our last season's itinerary we choose the Rondaxe Road entry on a spring day following months of snow runoff and relentless rainfall. Needless to say, the bridge at North Street doesn't clear by much...perhaps a foot. Does that stop us from trying to "run" under it? Of course not! However, one of us (namely one of the authors of this proviso) experiences an unintentional rollover in the process, losing (again) everything that wasn't tied down or contained in the drybag. How many cameras and binoculars must one sacrifice to the rivergods before learning?! The river is deep here, and when it is moving rapidly, strong swimming skills are needed, as well as buddies with long paddles.

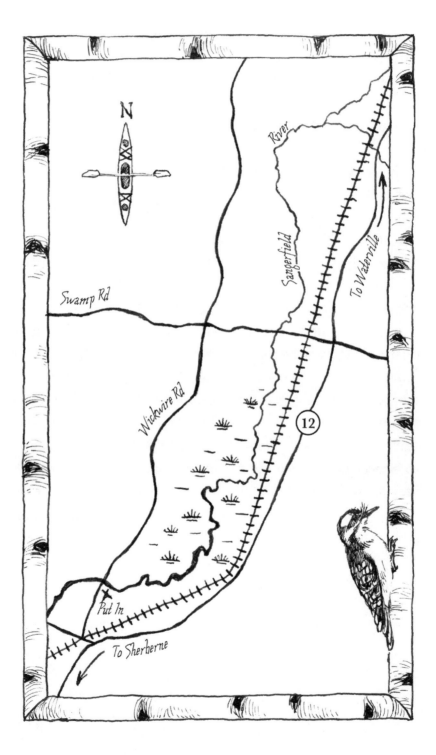

Nine Mile Swamp

The Nine Mile Swamp...home to the notorious family of thieves, arsonists, and murderers known as the Loomis Gang, who dominated the landscape during the 1800s when the area was wild and unsettled.

THE WAY THERE: Follow Route 12 south of Waterville and turn right onto Wickwire Road near Hubbardsville. Cross the railroad tracks and park near the bridge over the Sangerfield River (it's a well-established fisherman's parking area). The launch and take-out area is a gently sloping bank on either side of the bridge. Paddle upstream toward Swamp Road.

REFLECTIONS ON THE WATER: We embark for a few hours of quiet exploration on this narrow, placid stream, the usual chatter muted as the flotilla is forced to wend its way single file.

As we paddle, it would appear that little has changed in this seemingly desolate area, and we peer into the surrounding forests, looking for likely hiding places for the stolen horses, livestock, and other plunder that was brought in by the offspring of George Washington Loomis. The stream meanders through the uncleared swampland extending from Sangerfield Center to Hubbardsville, and we try to imagine the avenues of escape as a team of vigilantes closed in on the rascals.

With only the sound of an occasional turtle slipping off her log or the drumming of a woodpecker in search of a meal, we're alone with our thoughts. As mothers, we wonder at the history of the Loomis family, particularly Rhoda, the mother who oversaw a family of four girls, six boys, and innumerable servants and other young people who came and went in the old mansion. The stories of the family at home are intriguing, describing a devout, Bible-reading matriarch who admonished her boys as they were about to leave the house to "not come back without stealing something, if it's nothing but a jackknife." The daily fruits of their plunder would be placed upon the table, and the procurer of such would be praised and rewarded accordingly. Ah, motherhood, indeed.

The gentle stream lulls us as it leads us up the Chenango Valley toward the site of the old farm and mansion. The idyllic setting that opens up before our boats belies the turbulence that took place here only a few generations ago.

Willows overhang our path, and these, along with alders, maples, ash, cherry, aspen, and various and sundry conifer, envelop us in a continual aura of greenery as we journey toward the Swamp Road crossing. This will mark the halfway point of our trip, as navigating further would be difficult. So we carefully turn our little skiffs around, and see it all again, albeit in reverse – but not any less beautiful.

One of our daughters has joined us today. Gretchen is becoming more comfortable on the water with her mom and her "older" friends. We love to have her, and we hope that one day she'll be leading the rest of our daughters through these beautiful channels, sharing new stories with them.

DIVERSIONS: Birds will be calling from shore to shore, depending upon the season and time of day. Of course, if you're chattering with each other, as we usually are, you'll miss the conversations going on in the trees above. A true bird-watcher, however, will listen carefully and relish the variety of calls in this swampland wilderness.

CONSIDERATIONS: You will probably be eating lunch in your boat, as there is little opportunity to disembark throughout the journey. Water may be low if the summer months have been particularly dry, which could cause problems navigating through beaver dams and blowdown.

IS IT WORTH THE TRIP? This is a relatively easy paddle, with some intriguing history thrown in for good measure – all told, an enjoyable day on the water. I would recommend several trips, taken in different seasons, in order to see and appreciate the river and all it has to offer (and did offer to those notorious scoundrels of yesteryear). Familiarize yourself with their story, and the images will enhance every stroke of your paddle throughout this journey.

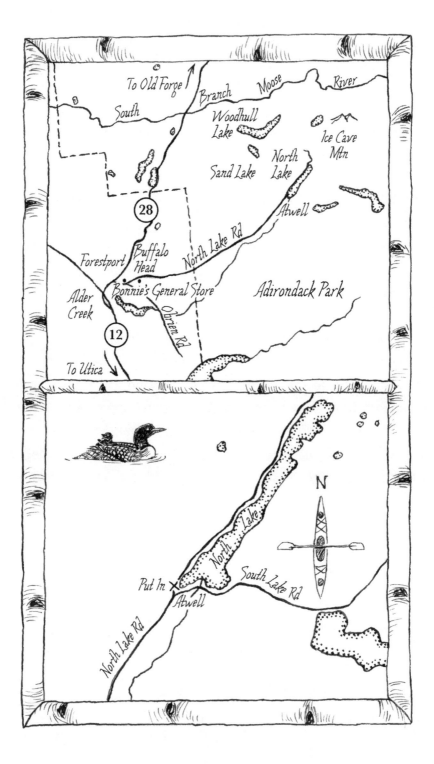

North Lake

Ladies, bring a friend, bring two, stay the night. Make your own fun.

THE WAY THERE: North Lake is fifteen miles past the Buffalo Head Restaurant in Forestport. Plan ahead for your needs, as the road can be relatively lonely and there are no gas stations past Alder Creek on Route 12 and no provisions after Bonnie's Country Store in Forestport Station. As you approach Atwell, you will see a bridge ahead. Turn left just before the bridge and park. Alternate parking is available at one of several casual, primitive campsites on the very rutty road that continues on up the lake. Park, lift your kayak over the rocks, and climb in.

REFLECTIONS ON THE WATER: North Lake is part of the Black River, stopped up by an earthen dam which is also the roadbed. It is about three miles long, narrow, and has camps mostly on the eastern side. There are a couple of small islands right offshore in downtown Atwell, with camps on the right, campsites on the left. One very interesting feature is that when the lake is low, many of the small islands seem supported by cobblestones.

We paddle up the east side, which is dotted by a number of

lean-tos. We stop at one, and pull out for a break and to nose around. This lean-to is totally ready for the next campers, outfitted with a roll of foil, matches, a grate for the fire pit, a deck of cards, and log stools. Almost ready, that is: it needs a corkscrew. I make a mental note to provide one. As a group, we make up stories about those before us who have furnished it so completely.

Butts back in our boats, we paddle up an inlet and listen to the water rush over rocks and into the lake. Then on to the far end, where we pull out for awhile and share our feast. Sandwiches, red peppers, celery, hummus, plums, cut melon, and Bonnie's soupy miniature peanut butter cups. I recall the time I sat in this exact spot for a half-hour in the rain watching a loon dive and pop up repeatedly.

There is a logging road nearby that leads to a trail to Ice Cave Mountain where there reportedly is – you guessed it – an ice cave, a break in the rocks so deep that the ice never melts. I have not found it.

We board our kayaks for our return. The sun is on our shoulders as we paddle along the opposite shore. There are two women on a dock, and we strike up a conversation. They and a friend are on a "chick trip," a yearly excursion. We move on again, heading into a cove where a loon approaches us. We decide that it is nesting and wants us out of there. We obey.

After a bit we decide to take an icy dip at an island near the center of the lake. Bonnie spontaneously directs a water ballet. It is not easy. We are to form a star. Six women holding hands, legs wide and feet touching. On the count of three, we all throw our bodies back and float. Or at least, that's what we're *supposed* to do! Take one: We fail to arch our backs and our butts sink. Take two: We fail to arch our backs; butts sink. Take three: We arch our backs but laugh so hard we lose our grip. Take four: Not bad.

We suddenly hear a dog yipping and realize we have interrupted a woman and her mop-headed dog attempting to enjoy some solitude on the other side of the island.

I feel this is the lake where the WOW group first really bonds. Women pulling boats from the tops of their cars, two more picking them up, lifting them over rocks until there are nine in our flotilla. Bonnie, Ruth, Joan, Betty, Judy, Carol, Anna, Mimi, Kathy. We paddle, some of us talking, others silent, moving forward, falling back, chatting with one, then another, Carol telling stories, Bonnie directing water ballet, Judy taking pictures, Betty speaking of remote and exotic destinations, everyone sharing lunch and soaking up the sunshine. We planned to take three hours, linger the day. Just a few old girls on boats...We floats.

DIVERSIONS: In addition to kayaking, the area offers hiking, camping, and caving. There are many trails in the vicinity. From the parking area, you can get to Sand and Woodhull Lakes or the South Branch of the Moose River. Stone Dam can be reached via a trail on the North Lake Road. For geocachers, there is only one listed cache, last found in 2005, so it is a ripe spot for more.

CONSIDERATIONS: North Lake is rather remote. Make sure you have gas, food, and water. Cell phone contact is iffy. The outhouse in Atwell is locked.

IS IT WORTH THE TRIP? Yes. I would also consider camping for a day or two, as there is so much more to do than kayaking.

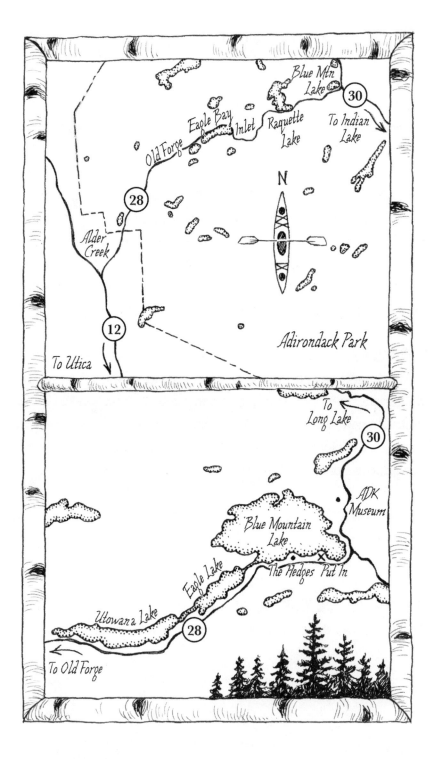

Blue Mountain Lake

THE WAY THERE: Blue Mountain Lake is located eighty-five miles north of Utica. Travel Route 12 north from Utica. At Alder Creek, bear right onto Route 28. Continue through Old Forge, Eagle Bay, Inlet, and Raquette Lake. Blue Mountain Lake is located at the junction of Route 28 and Route 30. You may launch your kayak at the public beach, but you will have to park on the road. There are bathroom facilities at the beach.

REFLECTIONS ON THE WATER: A Greek philosopher once said, "Many receive advice, few profit by it." When you hear "Blue Mountain Lake may be windy," heed the advice. I have checked and rechecked the forecast – sunny and a gentle six-mile-per-hour wind, it said. When we arrive, the lake is already tossing up white caps. So much for the forecast. We don our life preservers and head across the lake to investigate the far shoreline. We pass a blue and white float plane whose engine looks like a large mushroom extending above the cockpit.

The scenery is gorgeous. Blue Mountain lies in the background, and there are acres of balsam and pine – as far as the eye can see. White birch trees intersperse the green; rocky islands dot the horizon. We spot gulls, kingfishers, and possibly an eagle. Huge Adirondack camps are evident, many with cedar shake roofs and fieldstone fireplaces.

The "gentle breeze" has picked up fairly rapidly to a light gale. I am not as strong a paddler as Audrey, and although I am in my newer kayak, she is already a quarter-mile ahead of me. We try to hug the shoreline to escape the wind, with little success.

One could spend an entire day investigating Blue Mountain Lake, but our destination is Eagle Lake. We paddle under a picturesque wooden bridge constructed by Thomas C. Durant, founder of the Adirondack Railroad, and enter Eagle Lake, accessible only by water. All shoreline is posted property, owned by an artist's colony and private camps. At the end of the lake, a pristine, winding Adirondack river allows access to Utowana Lake.

We pass four men and two women in kayaks. "The Utowana is angry today. We're turning around," they holler. As we enter the

Adirondack architecture

lake, it looks like the ocean during a hurricane. The wind is howling and waves are crashing over my bow. But we continue paddling, our goal to investigate the bog at the end of the lake.

It starts to rain, and I don the dollar poncho that I keep in my boat. I have forgotten the rain skirt for my kayak, and water splatters down my legs. Audrey is using her cockpit cover for protection. I discover that what I believe is fog is just my glasses misting over. We pass two men in canoes seeking shelter under low-hanging pine branches. They are waiting out the rain and laugh at our bedraggled appearance.

We reach the bog. A lean-to and sandy beach appear through the light rain. Flowers are everywhere – pickerel weed, horned bladderwort, water lilies, spatterdock, and red sundew just starting to blossom. A kingfisher announces our arrival. We hear chickadees, wrens, sparrows, and cedar waxwings in the distance.

It's late, so we turn around and head back via the same route. The wildness of Utowana Lake contrasts with the sound of traffic from Route 28. We make one quick paddle up an inlet to a waterfall and notice on our way out that the wind has cut to nothing. So much for riding the waves back to shore. We pass several fishermen on a party barge that was in our vicinity when we launched many hours earlier. "You've had a good workout today!" they exclaim.

We enter Blue Mountain Lake and pass The Hedges, an Adirondack lodge. Two sisters are jumping off the dock into the clear water. As we make our way to shore, Audrey checks her GPS. We have paddled sixteen miles in seven-and-a-half hours, more than half of it into a brisk headwind. I almost wish that I had heeded the advice and chosen a dead calm day.

We load the kayaks and head to Inlet. Over a raspberry and vanilla gelato, I analyze today's outing – certainly challenging but worth every minute!

DIVERSIONS: A definite must-see is the renowned Adirondack Museum, often referred to as the "Smithsonian of the Adirondacks." The museum, opened in 1957, was created by mining magnate Harold Hochschild, who summered at nearby Eagle Lake as a child. Currently, the museum houses twenty-two exhibits on thirty-two acres overlooking the lake. The Adirondack guide boats themselves are worth the trip. You can also hike up Blue Mountain, a steep climb of 3759 feet. The view from the fire tower is priceless. Note that each of these excursions takes almost all day.

CONSIDERATIONS: Always plan ahead. Check the forecast. Experienced kayakers may not have a problem facing the wind, but novices can tire easily. Pack raingear and a skirt for your cockpit. Use a waterproof bag for gear. Large waves, especially from passing motorboats, should be faced head-on. Wear your lifejacket!

IS IT WORTH THE TRIP? For the intrepid, yes. Although the wind can be taxing, the scenery is spectacular.

Blue Mountain haze

Swimming lessons

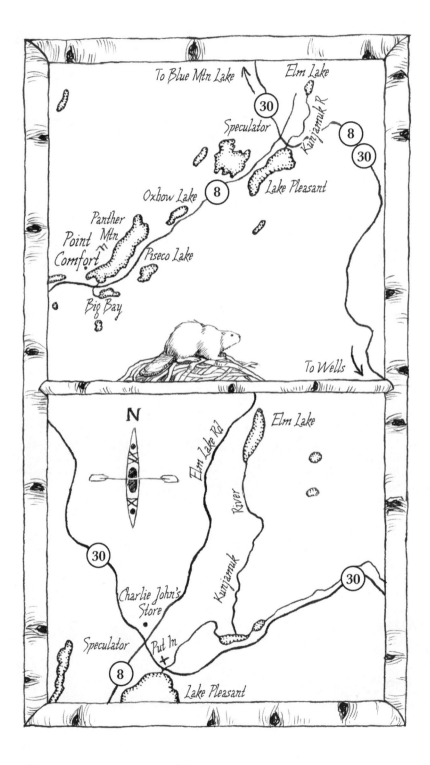

Kunjamuk River

THE WAY THERE: Take Route 8 north. It's a nice change of pace for us, this ride, as we generally access the Adirondacks via Route 28. Different lakes lure us: should we paddle Oxbow, we wonder, or head beyond the bridge on Piseco? But today we continue on to Speculator's town beach, where we plan to put in. We recognize others from our usual caravan of kayak-topped cars in the ample parking area across the street from the beach. This is also the parking lot for the pavilion that will host the Brooks Barbecue tonight, an event with which we've deliberately timed this week's paddle.

REFLECTIONS ON THE WATER: You'll find everything on the Kunjamuk – quiet water, steady streams, beaver dams, heron, turtles, mink, your friends, your inner peace, your soul. Though this is not a paddle for true beginners, we have brought one along. We set out, a large group – news of WOW has trickled through sports equipment establishments, at family reunions. More and more women join us on a weekly basis. We meet. We board our boats. We paddle northward.

This is a river some of our group have paddled before. Today we all are determined to navigate it, to reach its terminus: Elm

Lake. We have a new member, more experienced, who does not turn back at the sight of the first beaver dam blocking our route. No. When the rest of us turn the bend of the lazy upstream river, there is Audrey, her bi-colored boat already on the other side, and she, perched atop the dam, hauls each of us up and over as we aim our rapid paddle her way. She does not turn back at the sight of the second beaver dam, either, or the third, the fourth, we lose count; she just coaches us through, around, over, and out of our boats to portage them.

It is a lengthy and more challenging trek than we are accustomed to on a Thursday. Lunch at a bridge finds us only halfway there. Jude dozes, stretched out inside her kayak, and those with other obligations head back downstream. But some of us are committed. The second half is either less difficult or we've grown used to sharing the water with beavers.

Entry into Elm Lake is worth any effort. It's like crossing a border to a fairy tale. A misty river scene. We are alone on a still lake, deep, deep in the wilderness. We don't disembark, don't mar the magic of it all, just float, amazed, across the quiet expanse, measuring our blessings in an afternoon sun, the call of a cardinal, the splash of a fish tail.

We cannot linger long, though. The day trudges on, and we've a long paddle back. Downstream beaver dams, though, are pure fun. We Indiana Jones ourselves over the tops of them. We hoot and holler. We share our extra food. (On this long of a paddle – 12.2 miles by Audrey's GPS system – we decide we might have brought along two lunches.) But by the time we are back in familiar waters, the aroma from the barbecue comes wafting up, leading us home, tricking us into believing we are closer than we are.

Just before we enter the final leg of the river to the bridge, a side current slides into the mainstream, momentarily shifting the current, and giving us real bragging rights: we paddled more than twelve miles today, and upstream both ways!

It is with tired bodies we climb out of our kayaks, load our boats, soak our sandy feet and dip our sunburned shoulders in the swimming area across the street, then amble back for barbecue and scrumptious desserts. Fuel for the long ride home.

DIVERSIONS: Speculator is a good little town to mosey about. The Speculator Department Store carries clothing and gifts. Charlie Johns Store is fun to poke around in and boasts a formidable collection of Adirondack literature. There are several restaurants in the area. Lake Pleasant offers an a beach for swimming, and just a short trek back down Route 8 brings you to Point Comfort State Park, from which you can access a trailhead to hike Panther Mountain.

CONSIDERATIONS: Since this is such a long paddle, you will need to set aside a lot of time and carry plenty of water and a substantial lunch (or two). And go in a group.

IS IT WORTH THE TRIP? Absolutely, if you want to be mesmerized and are willing to be muscle-sore.

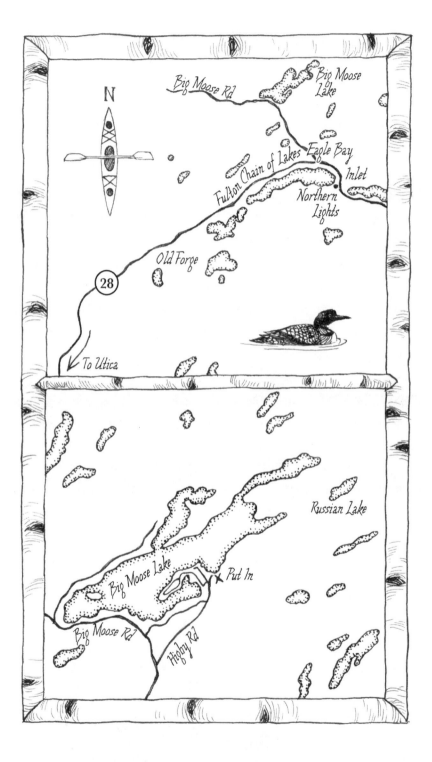

13 Big Moose Lake

"This is the best thing I've ever done in my whole life!" An eighteen-year-old "friend of a grandson" joins us for the day and learns to skinny-dip in a brisk mountain lake...hardly the typical trip description!

THE WAY THERE: Drive north of Old Forge on Route 28 until you reach the Big Moose Road near Eagle Bay. Turn left and continue approximately four miles on this road to Higby Road, where you will turn right and drive one and a half miles to the Big Moose Association launching site. Park so as not to block residents' cars.

REFLECTIONS ON THE WATER: On a day that threatens thunderstorms, we set out for Big Moose Lake and the scene of Theodore Dreiser's famous novel, *An American Tragedy*. We are surprised to find that the largest group of the summer (eighteen was the magic number on this day) has also ventured forth. Today's launch site, by agreement of the owner, is at The Big Moose Inn, a rustic and beautiful lodge and restaurant on the shores of this scenic body of water.

As we paddle away from the shoreline of the sparsely populated

photo by Bonnie Sanderson

Summer idyll

resort area (what a difference from the nearby Fulton Chain), we are greeted by a choir of loons, cooing and calling to each other for their own meeting, whose purpose is a mystery. There are so many of them together (we count nine in one group – note the dividend of our number of the day) that Shirley, a birder, thought the recent cold weather may have triggered a preparatory gathering for the annual southern migration. This is truly an unusual sight, as loons are very territorial and even drive off their young upon reaching adulthood. For a long time, we watch them dive and surface helter-skelter as they pursue their dinner in the depths of the lake.

The bays and outlets are serene, and the lake is only disturbed by a few fisherman and vacationing skiers who hope to satisfy their thirst for water activity before the oncoming storm. The homes and cottages along the shore blend into the surrounding forest landscape, so unlike those on many of the lakes that we have paddled. It appears that generations of inhabitants have adapted their lives and homes to the beauty of the Adirondacks instead of changing the mountain scenery into their own scheme. The area is historically significant for its unique architecture, utilizing vertical half-log construction in many of the lodges and cabins.

Karen, a newcomer to the group, tells us about Russian Lake, which is connected to the very end of Big Moose by a three-quarter-mile hike. A docking area allows us to disembark, leave our kayaks, and continue the journey by foot through a well-trimmed wilderness, meeting only one large family group along the way. We eat our lunch in the warmth of a sunny spot which even boasts a lean-to and fireplace.

The lake beckons, and several of the girls go for a cold, but refreshing dip in the dark, clear water. One old girl who hasn't worn a bathing suit on this day decides that it's just too inviting, and since it's such a remote wilderness area, swims in her birthday suit, wrinkled as it is! Meagan, our young WIT (WOW in training), finally is convinced that it's OK, and as she cautiously swims from the protection of the rocks, is heard singing out loud and clear, "This is the BEST THING I've ever done...these women are THE BEST!"

As we hike back to Big Moose Lake and continue our journey by boat, we look furtively about for the area where the 1906 murder of Grace Brown took place and the alleged ghost sightings have occurred. When the centennial of the event was observed, these claims brought renewed notoriety to the lake, and Dreiser's novel based on the murder and trial, as well as the subsequent movie, "A Place in the Sun," was revisited.

The storm clouds are gathering, so we return along the same route with greater urgency to avoid the oncoming thunder and lightning. We're just in time, and on our homeward journey, are

photo by Bonnie Sanderson

Hurrying home

reminded that we can't allow the meteorologist to "rain on our parade." This day will definitely be remembered.

DIVERSIONS: The homemade gelato at Northern Lights at the head of Arrowhead Park in Inlet is not to be missed! The flavors are changed frequently, and we haven't found one that hasn't pleased our palate. There are shops, museums, and a water-amusement park in the nearby Old Forge-Inlet vicinity if one is inclined to escape the quiet of the lake and forest. (Why on earth would one be so inclined?)

CONSIDERATIONS: The lake is approximately three miles long and one mile wide, varying in depth from twenty-three to seventy feet. Therefore, it can be difficult to paddle under windy conditions; wakes from boats and skiers can be a concern as well. Lifejackets should definitely be worn whenever there is risk of an upset.

IS IT WORTH THE TRIP? For sure. Its remote beauty is truly representative of Adirondack lakes as they have existed for centuries, and its relative peace and quiet will feed your soul. A reading of Dreiser's novel or a viewing of the film starring Elizabeth Taylor, Montgomery Clift, and Shelley Winters will stimulate your imagination and enhance your visit.

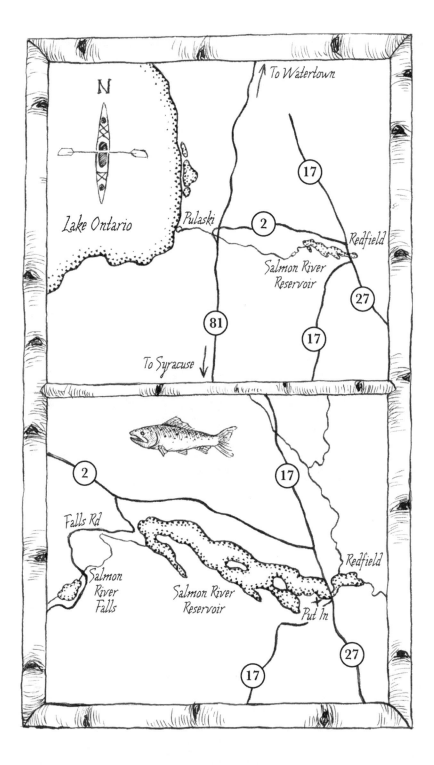

Salmon River Reservoir

THE WAY THERE: Take Route 49 from Utica to Rome, Route 69 from Rome to Camden, then Route 13 north. In Williamstown, take a right onto Route 17. The put-in is at the intersection of Routes 17 and 27. There is plenty of parking but no bathroom facilities.

REFLECTIONS ON THE WATER: Heraclitus once said, "You can't step twice into the same river." No matter the time or weather, paddling Salmon River Reservoir is always a unique experience. Flora and fauna change with the seasons, as does the difficulty of the trip.

The put-in is one of the easiest of all of our paddles. We need only to carry the kayaks twenty feet down a slight decline. The lake is seven miles long and at this time of morning, completely flat. Blue mountains and pine trees appear in the distant mist. We are not kayaking the lake today but rather the marsh, accessible by paddling under the bridge. By this time of year, we are adept at unloading boats and placing dry bags in kayaks. In no time, we set off under sunny skies and white cumulus clouds.

We pass houses, camps, and docks. Around a corner lies what appears to be a cottage with old school equipment in the yard.

The red, white, and blue merry-go-round, red slide, and green and white swings are empty this morning but show past use.

We paddle by a profusion of pickerel weed and water lilies and enter one of the side streams. The banks narrow appreciably and the current becomes stronger. Beaver and muskrat slides slice through the tall grass, and cedar waxwings abound, swooping overhead in search of insects. We paddle hard towards a gravel sandbar, our lunch spot for the day. Just as we are finishing sharing fresh fruit and stories, an unfamiliar kayaker from upstream misjudges the corner and dumps her boat in the deeper water. She makes her way across the stream, swamped kayak in tow. We discover that she is French and that this is her first time paddling. She disrobes and we hand her towels and sweatshirts to warm her. She says that she is lucky to be wearing her life preserver because she is not a strong swimmer.

Heading downstream after this drama, we pass into the larger section of the lake where the water depth varies considerably. Red maples survive well on small grassy islands; sugar maples show just a bit of color change. The teachers in our group exclaim in unison, "But we're not ready for school yet!" Adding to that sentiment is the chirp of numerous chickadees, to us a winter bird fond of sunflower seeds at the feeder.

We veer off into a bay and discover "pods" under the surface of the water. We have seen these bizarre products of nature before on other paddles but have yet to investigate their origin. The large and small gelatinous blobs are attached to branches and weeds. We raise a heavy one with our paddles and examine the interior. Not more than five minutes later, we encounter two biologists from Massachusetts who are fishing from their canoe. They tell us that the pods are actually bryozoans, also known as "water brains." There are fresh water and salt water varieties, with the fresh water type growing to almost basketball size. Bryozoans live in colonies and filter the water. Mystery solved.

Salmon River Reservoir is perimeter paddling at its best. We see a doe standing in the water, staring at our motley-colored kayaks. A juvenile bald eagle circles overhead, and herons ascend as we turn a corner. The birders in the group also spot king birds, osprey, and kingfishers. Because the water is high, we zigzag through willows and maples, quite alive even though trunks are submerged in water.

As we return to the bridge, the chop is evident. The reservoir is noted for its afternoon wind, and as we head up the lake proper, waves break over the bows of our kayaks. We put in at a small beach in order to swim, knowing that we will not attempt to tackle

Osprey in flight

the main part of the lake this afternoon. We paddle towards the parking lot, riding the waves into shore. We all agree that Salmon River Reservoir is definitely a repeat destination. There is still so much to discover.

DIVERSIONS: Travel down Route 2 to Orwell and turn onto County Route 22 south. Continue until you see a left turn for Falls Road. Follow the road to the Salmon River Falls parking lot; a sign indicates a New York State "Unique Area." The 110-foot falls is accessible by two trails, one above the water and onto the rocks, and the other, the "Gorge Trail," a switchback that ends at the bottom of the waterfall. Signage informs hikers about the area, the falls, and the reservoir. You can also hike up to the Salmon River Falls dam.

CONSIDERATIONS: If you are heading out on the reservoir, remember that the wind picks up in the afternoon.

IS IT WORTH THE TRIP? Absolutely! I have paddled Salmon River Reservoir three times, each one a unique experience.

Double exposure

Ladies' lunch

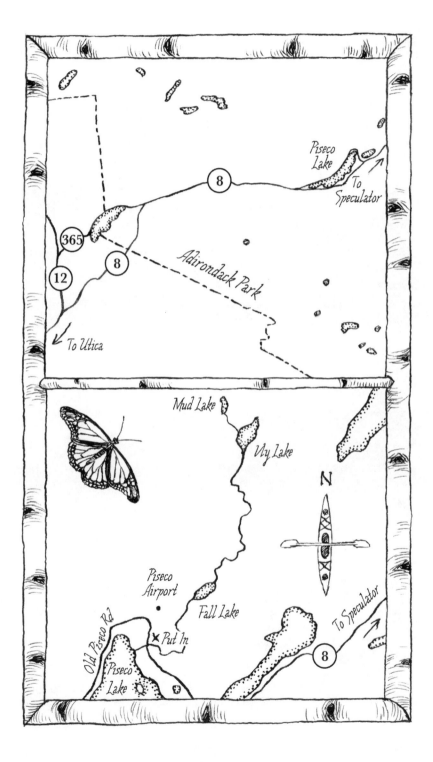

Piseco Lake

To Speculator

8

365

12

8

To Utica

Adirondack Park

Mud Lake

Uly Lake

Piseco Airport

Fall Lake

N

Old Piseco Rd

Put In

Piseco Lake

To Speculator

8

Fall Lake, Vly Lake, Mud Lake

THE WAY THERE: Piseco Lake, fifty-four miles north of Utica, is your destination for this paddle. Take Route 12 north from Utica and exit at Route 365. Head east to Route 8, then turn left and travel to Piseco. Take another left at the sign for Piseco Lake Airport. The launch area is on your right after a small bridge. Parking is limited, and there are no bathroom facilities.

REFLECTIONS ON THE WATER: We plan to spend the day in the Adirondack wilderness on this thirteen-mile round trip paddle. Once again, the WOW group is out in force, with ten of us willing to ford numerous beaver dams to get to our destination.

We unload the kayaks and walk down a small decline to set the boats in the water. A helpful kayaker has placed wooden boards over the dark mud to enable us to launch our boats with little problem. We set off upstream.

This trip is a wildflower aficionado's dream. Pickerel weed abounds on both sides of the twenty-foot-wide stream. Sea beach rose is in abundance, as is buttonbush, common elder, and pitcher plant. Wildlife is evident too – we pass turtles basking in the sun and great blue herons still as statues.

As we round a corner, we hear the sound of running water – beaver dam number one. It is a small one that can be forded without leaving the kayak. Farther along, I hear a noise behind me and discover two fishermen in a blunt-nosed duck boat heading upstream for Mud Lake and some bass fishing. As they pass, I watch them gun the motor and leap over beaver dam number three with no problem. Unfortunately, I do not have the same success. I realize that the fishermen have come just at the right time. After my third attempt to conquer the fast-moving current, they throw me a rope, put the boat in forward, and in a snap, I am over the dam and under my own power once again.

Our group meets in a calm spot and discusses various techniques to ford the thirteen beaver dams. Stronger-armed kayakers can pull themselves over most of the dams, but many of us have to disembark either by the edge of the overgrowth or on the dam itself in order to haul the boat over and then work our way back into the cockpit without dumping into the fast moving water.

As the day progresses, we become more successful. The wildlife, flowers, and mountains in the distance make us forget the difficulties of this excursion. We pass eight-foot-tall beaver houses but see no sign of the residents themselves.

We enter Vly Lake and notice cedar waxwings and turkey vultures. Pine-covered mountains surround us. We head for the end of the lake and our lunch spot, a campsite complete with grill. A covered, white pail catches our attention and inside we discover, floating in water, a map of the three lakes. Off to our left, a bright orange mushroom sits in moss. We take pictures but don't touch.

Replenished, we head for Mud Pond. Labrador tea with its pink flowers and fruit abound. We catch sight of arrowhead and spotted jewelweed, which is reputed to be a remedy for poison ivy.

Note to self: bring bailer

Cardinal flowers are resplendent in their bright red, and their reflection in the water looks computer generated.

We reach Mud Pond and find the two fishermen happily ensconced in their boat, hoping for the "big one." We are deep in the Adirondacks, a place most of the population will never find.

As we start our return, a great blue heron perches on a dead tree pruning his feathers, not caring that ten women are viewing his progress. We scoot over several of the smaller beaver dams but at the largest one, I run into trouble. I am the one that says, "I am NOT getting out of my kayak again" and thus I teeter on the four-foot-high dam, only to slowly but surely tip over into the dark and smelly water. The disaster is reminiscent of the *Laugh-In* comedy show where Arte Johnson falls over with his tricycle. I stand in muck up to my knees and water to my waist. The only item I have to bail with is a yogurt cup, and it takes me twenty minutes to scoop out the black water from my kayak. Note to self:

Gathering nectar

bring a sponge or buy a bailer for future trips.

None the worse for wear, we continue back to the launch site with monarch butterflies accompanying us as we kayak down the current. It has been a magnificent day, one of the best paddles of the year.

DIVERSIONS: You can plan a quick trip to Speculator, just north of Piseco. High on Page Hill, the Melody Lodge serves lunch and dinner with a commanding view of Lake Pleasant. In town, The Inn at Speculator offers year-round dining. The Speculator Department Store and Charlie Johns Store are a must stop for all sorts of Adirondack goods.

CONSIDERATIONS: The entire trip will take you several hours, but you can shorten the excursion by not traveling up to Mud Lake. Fall Lake is beautiful, as is Vly Lake. Note that there are numerous

Reflected beauty

beaver dams. Novice kayakers need to practice on small beaver dams before attempting the bigger ones!

IS IT WORTH THE TRIP? Definitely! Bring your wildflower book in a dry bag so that you can identify the numerous flora.

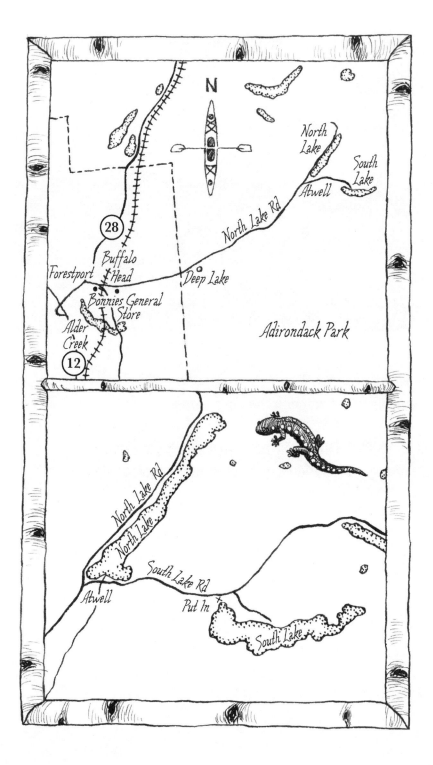

South Lake

THE WAY THERE: The journey to South Lake starts a short distance east of Route 28 north of Utica at the Buffalo Head in Forestport Station. Take the left fork and follow North Lake Road for seventeen miles. Electrical service ends at the sawmill just past Deep Lake. Drive on as the pavement turns to dirt. Continue on to Atwell on the west end of North Lake, cross the earthen dam, and in three more miles, voila!

REFLECTIONS ON THE WATER: There are a few primitive campsites on the right and a blue boathouse. I have parked at both. An alternate put-in is the Dodge-Pratt-Northam Park on the right just past the painted rock.

South Lake beckons me for many reasons. My great aunt Kathryn was born in 1891, the youngest of five girls. She, like her sisters, left the farm in her late teens to become a domestic for well-to-do families in Utica. She worked for Hobart Roberts, who was known for his wildlife photography. He had a camp on the south shore of the lake where he and his family would vacation, bringing along the household staff.

My normally timid aunt, finished with her child-rearing and

cleaning duties, assisted him in his nighttime endeavors. The process went like this: They would row the equipment down the lake in a guide boat and set baited lines near shore. When fauna attempted to take the bait, it would trip the line which would trigger flash powder, and Hobart would snap the picture from the boat. This sort of activity was uncharacteristic for Kathryn. She couldn't swim and was terrified by the instability of the loaded guide boat.

On this warm day in September, there is one other truck at the boathouse. We unload and are escorted into the water by a four-inch salamander and welcomed (or reproached) by three loons frantically yodeling.

We head on down the lake. Most of the camps and homes are on the north shore, three are opposite. At least two families are permanent residents – think generators and battery-operated appliances.

Looking toward the Roberts camp (still owned by descendents), where a small dwelling perches on piers over the water, I consider the ordeal of the drive from Utica in 1910, and of crossing the lake with a family, household help, food, and photographic equipment. We notice activity and paddle over to connect with the sons of sons, or in our case, the daughters of daughters, three generations hence.

Three miles down the lake, shores narrow as we pass through a channel that leads into another pond. It is remote and still and I float silently with a heron, a handful of dragonflies, and an occasional flip of a fin. This must be where Hobart and Kathryn set their lines. Jude and I continue on up the inlet with a little hindrance by beaver dams.

On the return trip to the car, we locate a primo picnic spot – the dam. There are a wooden dock, a shallow sandy area for a swim (or water ballet), and a trail that leads back around the lake or to Haskell Road in Noblesboro. The water is the source for the Black River; it leaves via a covered drain deep under the lake and is diverted to below the dam.

After a swim, as we paddle back to the truck, my mind wanders back to 1910, and I am hopeful that my dear old great-aunt Kathryn – who waited at the upstairs window for her stepmother to return for fear she would be left motherless again, who cowered from her gruff, overbearing father and endured open affairs by her husband – briefly betrayed her usual timid, fearful self and embraced her adventuresome self late at night in the remote dark waters at the far end of South Lake.

DIVERSIONS: This is a full-day trip. Should you decide to stay, neighboring North Lake has more campsites and lean-tos.

CONSIDERATIONS: Allow three hours for travel round trip from Utica, four hours for the paddle and play. Last gas is on Route 12 in Alder Creek, and the last provisions are at Bonnie's Country Store in Forestport Station. There is a privy at the Dodge-Pratt-Northam Park. Two caveats: black flies rule in June and big wind can come up quickly.

IS IT WORTH THE TRIP? Without a doubt. This lake is scenic, serene, and satisfying. Be sure to take your time and check out the coves. Hobart Roberts' wildlife photography can be seen in the dining room at the Kayuta Drive In on Route 12 in Alder Creek.

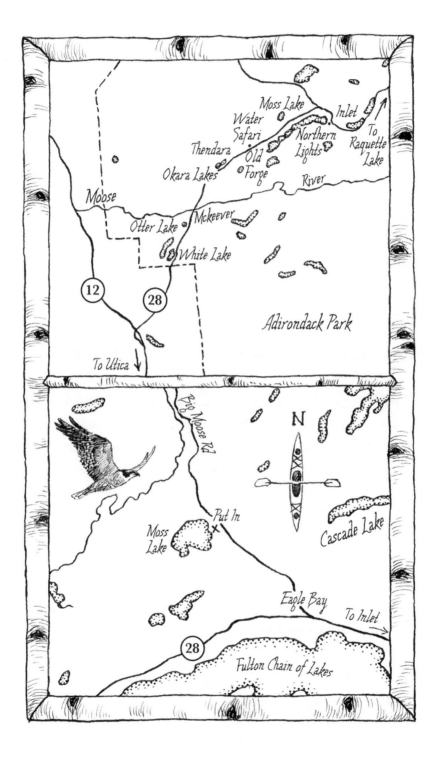

Moss Lake

In the company of waterfowl.

THE WAY THERE: The drive is doable, not cumbersome at all. Route 12 north from the Utica exit of the NYS Thruway brings you, after some twenty-five miles, to a V, the right side of which takes you along the newly expanded Route 28 north. You haven't gone far when you enter the Adirondack Park, with its yellow and brown signs signaling peace for those of us who cherish it. A winding ride slows your travel and your psyche enough to enjoy viewing the variety of camps.

Occasional glimpses of the lakes along the way keep you yearning to be afloat on those tannic waters. First White Lake, on the west side, opening in coves of beauty; then Otter, only visible between the cottages and trees. Next a sign informs of Okara (which means "the eyes") Lakes; they might "see" you, but you won't see them. You will cross the Moose River in McKeever and climb a small rise where, if you go in fall, you will find autumnal splendor to take your breath away! The Thendara Station means you are nearly to Old Forge. Slow down for the tourists and deer and glimpse the great shopping you can do after your paddle.

Beyond the Water Safari and Paul Bunyan's widespread gate of legs, you are back in the woods. Travel about eight miles to Eagle Bay. You'll spot the hamlet's one grocery store, after which you make the left onto Big Moose Road. It's not far now. Five minutes brings you to a trailhead for Cascade Lake on your right. Slow down. The Moss Lake parking lot is on the left, yards up the road. It is amply spaced. There is a small carry through refreshingly dark and cool woods to the put-in. (Apply bug spray before you venture in.)

REFLECTIONS ON THE WATER: Moss Lake is a paragon of utter peacefulness and unutterable beauty, dropped into the forest by a kind and loving God, removed, yet accessible to everyone. At first glimpse it will seem almost perfectly round, but as you paddle the shoreline you'll find the little niches that give this quiet water sport its simple ecstasies.

Mostly, though, you will spot the osprey nest on the island in the center of the lake. Depending on the season, you might spot the mother, white head with black cheeks, white breast, and blackish wings and back, or her babies, flapping their own wing feathers in readiness for their first flight. If you are especially blessed, or exceedingly attentive, you might even catch a glimpse of her fishing, hovering over the water, then plunging feet first to pluck lunch from the lake. But always the nest. Summer or winter. Spring and fall. In the uppermost branches. A sure and steady sign of a continued wilderness.

Paddling the lake puts you in the company of waterfowl if you come early and keep quiet. On our WOW visit a pair of loons approaches nearer our boats than any of us have ever thought possible, engaging in a diving dance that captivates us in their magic circle. Only cameras click. Are we floating atop a school of fish, or is Kathy's new kayak some sort of loon lure? Finally, while one bird submerges, the mate flaps his wings and skids across the water, away. On her return to surface, she looks, and looks, and looks. Neither she nor we can find him. Then, the magic of it stops the heart, a long black beak divides and the haunting, mesmerizing call echoes. Other loons respond from different shore spots – nests? But not the mate. We paddle on, newly knowledgeable in loon language and feather.

We navigate every inlet as far as possible along the shoreline, finding flora to admire. A photo shoot by the wooden bridge at the lake's far end halts us long enough for some to wonder if we could portage it and paddle the stream on the other side. Two kayakers go. The rest of us continue the course around the lake. The adventurers will return to tell us the side trip is a must. Two others will venture downstream. Then, after lunch on the observation post, three more of us. It is a tiny carry, just an up and

Footbridge on Moss Lake trail

over, really, and the stream is most appropriate for the smallest of groups. Bonnie, Carol, and I stop on the bridge to discuss the new ultra-light canoes beached by the couple resting on the wooden platform. Hers, a kind of kayak-canoe hybrid, weighs only ten pounds. Only ten pounds! Each of us in turn lifts it with an easy hand, utters the inevitable "wow!" We pause for a lesson on the factory, the creator, the advantages (obviously, the ease of carrying; she straps it over her shoulder for longer hauls, not much more cumbersome than my mother's purse!) and disadvantages (wind takes it a bit; the fabric is not as durable as our sturdy plastic kayaks, though they tell a story of a man whose boat was overrun by a tractor trailer; after its return to the shop, it has been remolded as good as new, the tire tread track down its middle making it a marvelous conversation piece as well as a wonderful boat).

We enter the stream. Solitude, serenity, and the absence of man's (and woman's) hand on the planet. We bask. At the log-jammed little falls, Carol disembarks and wanders down shore to explore the lower end a bit. She and Bonnie photograph each other from opposite sides of the falls.

On the way back, in the shallow waters before the bridge, Carol and I hear a sound like a baseball hitting the water; we look in time to see a kingfisher at work. Amazing.

DIVERSONS: Circling the lakeshore is a hiking trail. It is an old bridle path that circumnavigates the lake in a two-and-a-half-mile loop. Fairly level and generally wider than a typical trail (making it also a good cross-country ski or snowshoe trail), it passes within sight of the water, crosses quaint wooden bridges and treks off into the forest for samples of flora and scents of pine and cedar. Seven campsites are available along the shoreline, including at least one that is handicapped accessible. A platform has recently been built just beyond the boat put-in where paddlers and other visitors can enjoy a leisurely lunch and rest at the water's edge, osprey nest in full view.

For an after-paddle special treat, a five-minute drive on Route 28 will bring the kayaker to the village of Inlet, where just beyond the town park, at the Northern Lights outdoor ice cream stand, they sell homemade gelato in daily flavors ranging from pannicotta to Rafaello (a coconut and nut concoction) that transport the taster from the lakes of the Adirondacks to the canals of Venice in a single mouthful. Enjoy.

CONSIDERATIONS: The lake seems small at first glance, and the hiking trail short. Unfamiliar visitors might be inclined to schedule a brief stay. Though the confines of the lake can be kayaked or the trail trekked in probably an hour or so, the quick visit will not provide the true flavor of the place, which is all about losing time, freeing body and soul to drift on calm waters, the heartbeat to slow to the rhythm of the wind, the mind to meander smoothly like a loon, without considering time or the world beyond the borders of the lake, beyond the foot of the mountain, beyond the simplicity and satiety of earth, water, and sky. Give yourself the morning or the afternoon. Give yourself the day. It will be a present you'll savor later in traffic jams, at office meetings, in crowded buildings, waiting in line at grocery stores.

IS IT WORTH THE TRIP? Always. In any season and from anywhere!

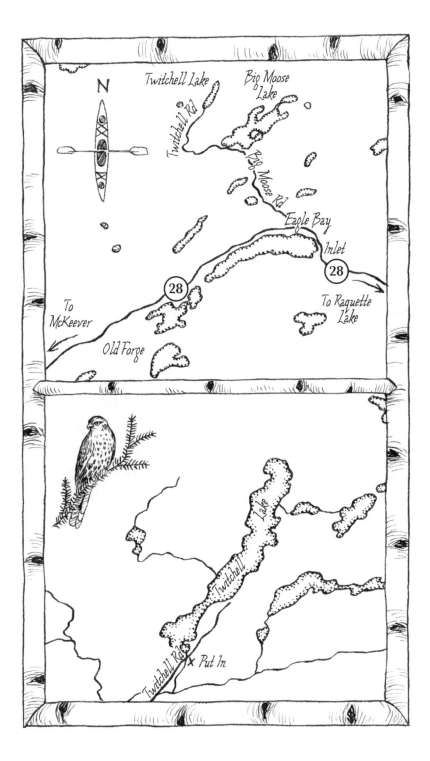

Twitchell Lake

THE WAY THERE: Driving to Twitchell Lake is a treat in itself as Route 28 winds through Old Forge and into Eagle Bay, where a left turn onto Big Moose Road takes you deeper into the wilderness. You pass Big Moose Lake, the Big Moose Inn, and the Big Moose Chapel, a historic stone church which is often the site of weddings. Several miles farther, turn right onto Twitchell Road, a paved road that soon turns into well-maintained dirt. The road ends at the lake, where there is ample parking and immediate access to the water. Note that there are no bathroom facilities.

REFLECTIONS ON THE WATER: Not five minutes into our paddle on Twitchell Lake, we hear the "kee-kee-kee" of a merlin perched in a tall pine. We know it is going to be another good day on the water.

There are eight of us today. Nancy is back after a two-year hiatus and she melds into the group as if she was never gone. Several of the kayakers are new, so first names are exchanged. We are happy to be on the water and to have escaped the heat of the city.

As we round the first corner, a woman hails us from her dock. "Are you the Moose River Paddlers?" she asks. We reply that we are the WOW group. "Oh! The WOW group!" she exclaims. She says that farther down the lake, a loon is nesting on an egg. Our resident birder, Audrey, informs us that this is a late nesting and that the chick may not make it off the water in the fall.

While some kayakers paddle in the middle of the lake, there are those of us who mosey along the shoreline. The lake is one and one-quarter miles long, but by investigating several nooks and crannies, you will clock about five miles by the end of the paddle. Perimeter paddling allows one to see nature at its best. On a grey, deserted dock, we spend five minutes watching a very large, black spider attempt to sneak up behind an iris-blue dragonfly only to have its dinner foiled at the last minute.

As we paddle down the lake, we notice that the camps are rustic brown or grey timber and set back from the water. In a previous trip to Twitchell, we learned that any newer construction must adhere to the Adirondack Park rules regarding distance to the water. Most residents also own a float with a small motor attached that allows them contact to parts of the lake not accessible by the one private road. Many of the floats do double duty as residents glide around the lake sitting in Adirondack chairs.

  We pass the Twitchell Lake Lodge, an Adirondack great camp built in 1899 by Earl Covey. The lodge and contents, including three moose heads, a Steinway piano, and several Covey tables, were auctioned off in 2009. At the far end of the lake, a sturdy lean-to houses a glass bookcase full of Adirondack books that may be borrowed by Twitchell Lake residents.

Finding a spot for lunch is sometimes difficult, as the lake has only private shoreline. But we have done this before, and eating on the water, floating together, provides time to catch up with family news and discuss possible future excursions.

As we head back to the launch site, we pass the loon sitting on her egg. She is easy to miss as she lies with her neck extended, close to the ground, appearing dead. We see her mate several times around the lake and hear his "oo-AH-ho" haunting call. Later I check the bird book and learn that loons usually nest on two olive-brown spotted eggs and that their feet are unusually far back on their body, thus allowing the birds to be expert divers, even to depths of two hundred feet.

A refreshing swim cools us before our trip back home. Twitchell is a symbiotic blend of nature, old camps, and history, a destination to which one should return.

DIVERSIONS: Inlet is a small but flourishing Adirondack village. Stops at Mary's White Pine Bakery and Gift Shop are essential. The Adirondack Reader is a fine book store, housing not only Adirondack books but also best sellers. If rain threatens, The Strand, Old Forge's movie theater, is a wonderful treat. View, the Old Forge arts center, has a premier watercolor competition each year and terrific exhibits year-round.

CONSIDERATIONS: The wind can come up on Twitchell in the afternoons, so novice paddlers may struggle to return to the launch site.

IS IT WORTH THE TRIP? Definitely! I have paddled Twitchell three times in the last year, and each is a new experience. Fall is especially gorgeous.

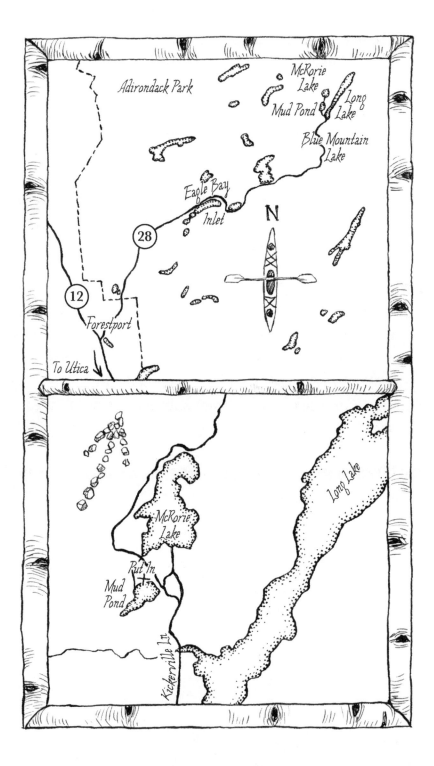

Mud Pond and (Nearly) McRorie Lake

"And I have waited two years for this?!" Sue exclaims as we admire the rocky shoreline from the forested bank.

THE WAY THERE: Seven of us meet in Forestport. After Artie's mandate to stop at The Donut Shop in Eagle Bay, we continue along Route 28 to Blue Mountain Lake, then on to Long Lake. From there we take Route 30 across the bridge over Long Lake, then the second right onto Kickerville Road. This is where our story begins.

REFLECTIONS ON THE WATER: For some misguided reason I am driving the lead car, and as the ride progresses there are ominous signs: PRIVATE ROAD; UNAUTHORIZED VEHICLES PROHIBITED; NO TRESPASSING. I stop, step out of the car, turn back to face Carol and shrug my shoulders. She gives me two flips of her hand, motioning me forward. In Carol-speak this means, "Yeah, yeah. Ignore the signs." Moving on, we cross a wooden one-lane bridge and see a sign for public parking, ignore that as well, and drive until we can drive no more. We have reached "the three gates." We have previously read about these portals: the right gate allows passage to private camps, the middle to Cedarlands, a Boy Scout Camp, and the left, the public access to Mud Pond and McRorie Lake. Carol has done some investigating and called the Boy Scout Council. The static-laced reply on her cell phone went something like this: "......locked......private access......mile......" Because the authorized trail to McRorie involves a one-mile portage or two one-third mile portages with a paddle on Mud Pond, we are desperately hoping the Cedarlands gate is open and some generous maintenance worker is willing to take pity on seven old ladies. There is a man in a maroon truck stopped at the open right gate. Carol jumps out of her car and rushes over to state our case. He politely but firmly explains that the ONLY WAY in is via the dreaded portage, locks the gate, and drives away.

We begin the unloading. I am still working on the J rack issue and now carry a three-step stool with me. I climb on the stool and as Gail, my recently retired sister, takes the back of my kayak, I carefully lift the front over the rack, remembering that last week Jude dropped her kayak and broke the driver's side mirror on her car. Some of us carry all seven boats around the left gate while others drive the cars back the one-third mile to the parking area. Robin returns with a note pulled off Audrey's windshield. "One mile" is the message.

Four of us have wheels, three do not. We decide that we will go as far as we can with all the kayaks, setting them down if we need to. The trail has a gentle uphill slope and we have not traveled a hundred yards before we come to a large open space.

"They could have put the parking lot here," someone grumbles. Unanimous agreement.

I call to Carol "Did you bring the map?"

"It's in my head," she replies.

"Swell."

Our arms feeling like they are being pulled from their sockets, we finally see the arrow-marked "TRAIL" pointing to the left. It is an easy downhill to Mud Pond. It has been an hour since we arrived.

Once in the water, we begin looking in all the obvious places for the passage or the trail marker to McRorie. We are not successful, so Gail climbs from her boat to a log to get a better vantage point – but still no clue. Hunger gets the best of us and out comes our food. Knowing ahead that this would be a demanding adventure, I have packed enough food for two days, and so has everyone else. This is one of those eat-as-you-float situations, and Sue, who has a relatively fragile, lightweight kayak, is moving perilously close to a downed pine with sharp broken branches that are poised to impale her vessel in the next stiff wind. Gail has baited her casting rod and now has her line in the water. As we chatter we drift, and Ruth muses that whatever happens, we are paddling on a lovely little pond. I am mentally doubling time and distance in our search for the elusive McRorie Lake when someone spies a yellow and red kayak and yells "Audrey!"

"It's Gail!" is the response from the distance. Carol takes this opportunity to spur us on to our destination. We agree to return to the trail and search on foot.

After paddling back and dragging our craft up the hill, we decide to leave everything until we know how far and how difficult the trail is. Artie notices Audrey's wheel tracks. Now in two groups, Ruth, Sue, and Carol ahead, Robin, Gail, Artie, and I bringing up the rear, we cross a bridge and note that if we could get past those boulders, it appears we might find McRorie Lake. But there is no indication of a trail on the other side of the bridge, so that can't be the way. A little farther on, there is an arrow made of rocks pointing into the woods.

Does this arrow mean something?

"Do you think Audrey did that?" Robin asks.

"It looks like it's been there too long," I reply, and on we go.

It's hot. We have been walking for forty minutes, Ruth, Carol and Sue are no longer in sight, and Audrey's wheel tracks have long since disappeared. "I walk three miles in an hour," Artie offers, and on we go.

Finally we see the lake through the trees. We stop to take a breather and see the others returning.

"Did you find the put-in?" Robin queries.

"Nope!" is the retort.

Sue suggests we at least go down to the shore, so the seven of us, figuring we can take a dip, make our way, stepping on sticks, trudging over downed trees, shrub branches lashing our legs until we get to the water's edge.

Swimming is not an option. There is a muck bottom with a matrix of dead branches that would need climbing over. The lake itself is beautiful, a bowl of water with a scalloped edge of mountains for a rim. Way off in the distance something appears to be floating. Could it be Audrey? No great whistlers among us, we yell in unison. "AUUUDDREEEE!" and hear our echo, "Auuuddreeee." This lung-wrenching exercise is repeated four more times before we are certain that Audrey has indeed heard our calls and is heading our way. As she approaches, she pulls out her camera and snaps a photo of us, boatless, at the edge of the elusive McRorie Lake. She had been camping with her parents (who are in their eighties) and arrived earlier, leaving blazes along her path. "Didn't you see the arrows I made with sticks and stones?" she asked.

As she makes her return paddle and we make our return hike, we meet at the three gates. There is a man who tells us that despite the no trespassing signs, the bridge is the entry to McRorie. Next time! We agree that we are hot, tired, and in need of a swim, and we decide to stop at the beach in Long Lake.

All of us have noted the beach as we've passed by, but none has taken the time to appreciate the raft at the park. In litigious New York State, here is a raft, lifeguardless, with a slide, a trampoline, and three rope swings. Three nine-year-old boys are taking full advantage of the amenities. Carol and Ruth are first into the bracing water. Gail and I follow. The lure of the raft is irresistible. We swim to it, climb the ladder and slide, swim to the raft, climb the ladder and bounce, swim to the raft, climb the ladder and... can't reach the ropes. The boys show us how. The receivers must be ready. Carol is poised. One boy jumps, hits the rope backwards; Carol realizes what she is expected to do, but is too late to grab the rope and stands forlorn on the raft. The next boy tells her she has to be ready to grab the rope, jumps, and slaps it back to Carol. Voila! Rope in hand, she catapults herself into the water and sends the rope back to Gail. Gail gets it and follows. I fail to grab the rope as it comes back to me, but a willing nine-year-old jumps and taps the line to my waiting arthritic hands. I am the third to make use of the delicious rope swing. We haven't done this in years, and our initial entries into the water from the raft are ungainly. Gail, however, has always had remarkable muscle memory, and each time she enters the water via the trampoline, her dives become more graceful. We continue to play as the others arrive. Artie, Audrey, Robin, and Sue. Sue has not worn a bathing suit, but despite the observers on shore, she jumps in wearing her shirt and bottoms, and joins the frolicking to cool her body in the lake. We enter the water as more-than-middle-aged women and surface like nine-year-old boys, gleefully immersed in the late summer pursuit.

Bodies cool, we discuss our options. We stop to peruse the books and gifts at Hoss's Country Corner before heading to Inlet for salted caramel gelato.

DIVERSIONS: Too many to list. Check the local papers for events.

CONSIDERATIONS: Bring a map.

IS IT WORTH THE TRIP? I'll be back – and better prepared.

The aquacar?

"AUDREEEEE!"

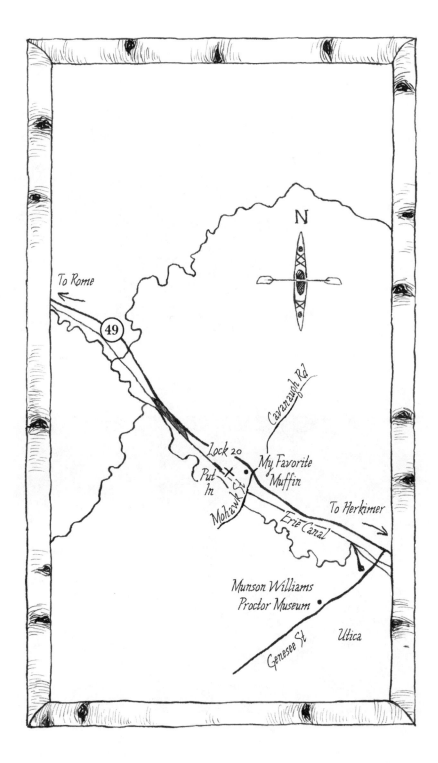

Erie Canal

"...and you'll always know your neighbor, and you'll always know your pal..."

THE WAY THERE: We put in at Lock 23 with advance permission of the lockkeeper. Accessed from Route 49 in Marcy, a short jaunt for most WOW members, this trip leaves ample pre-paddle time for breakfast in any of the area's friendly diners and cafes. We eat this morning at My Favorite Muffin and Bagel Café in the Marcy Plaza.

REFLECTIONS ON THE WATER: First of all, come prepared for a different kind of paddle, a thoroughly enjoyable, if less serene, outing. The Barge Canal is still regularly trafficked in the summer months, particularly at the start and end of the season, with large boats returning to or exiting the Great Lakes for venues further south. It's likely you'll share the lock. We don't, but we have called ahead to assure its availability for kayakers, to find out for certain how many boats needed to be ready for the filling or lowering, etc. I expect a wait is possible.

Beyond your particular mindset, there is an agility factor to consider. From the floating docks that line the banks of the canal, paddlers must make a deep-water boarding into their boats. This is fairly easily accomplishable for those who load first, trickier for the last paddler with no one left on land to steady her boat. (We solve this problem by bringing along the good-sport husband of one of our founding members to help, christening him an honorary woman on water. Walt's good nature extends to his meeting us at the end of our paddle – this will be a one-way expedition for us – to ferry us back to our cars, and to his patience with our frequent calls of, "Oh, Kayak-boy..." We treat him to lunch at Kitty's on the Canal for his efforts.) Still, a reasonably nimble kayaker could, with a bit of effort, ingenuity, and willingness to get wet, board her boat herself for the canal trek.

We wait for the lock to fill and the heavy doors to push open, and we float in. Each of the fifty-seven locks of the Erie Canal is 328 feet long, 45 feet wide. This seems like a big space, even for a dozen or more kayakers. The lockkeeper assures us he once sent twenty Boy Scouts in canoes down this same lock. When Kathy asks, "Were any of them seventy years old?" he acknowledges us with a smile. Inside, though, the lock looks considerably smaller, eerier, as the water level drops and your boat descends and you are afloat beside a slime-covered wall, an equally slimy rope in your palm, slipping ever downwards. I am very, very glad to see the rectangular patch of blue sky above me despite the fact that I am not prone to claustrophobia. The somber mood is broken for us when Kathy announces, "I'm at the end of my rope." Indeed, we all are. Moments later the opposite doors push open, and we glide into calm water, in clean air, free.

The paddle itself is leisurely and lovely, though quite noisy. Traffic sounds, shooting and fake distressed bird calls from a nearby farmer's field, construction work on the bridges underneath which we pass, all remind us we are paddling an age-old commercial thoroughfare, not a pristine Adirondack lake. We make a weak attempt at the Erie Canal song. We continue along the same straight pathway "kayak-yakking," as the waitress at Kitty's will call it later.

Goldenrod glints from the shrubbery lining the canal. Some leaves are already changing. Joggers pass us on the trail that runs along the southern rim. As we pass a moored tug, one of the men asks, "How far do you have to go?"

"Have to?" I wonder. Why, we are on our Thursday adventure. There is no have to today. Only want to.

And we want to do this: float in quiet boats on smooth waters; tell our stories to women who know and care; breathe in the molecules of independence, courage, and peace that drift in the air

photo by Bonnie Sanderson

"I'm at the end of my rope"

photo by Jude Dawes

Locked in

from the multitudes of women who've gone here, grown here before us; connect to the land, the water, and every bird and beast and wildflower with which we share this place of wonder.

"Looks like fun," a worker calls from the last bridge under which we pass.

"It is!" I call back.

It is FUN! Which is another thing we "few old girls" just want to have. Summers like we haven't had since we were ten years old.

The canal trip is our last summer expedition of our first year. School teachers among us will be back to work the following Thursday.

DIVERSIONS: Well, there's Utica. And everything it has to offer – Munson-Williams-Proctor Art Museum, great restaurants, the National Distance Running Hall of Fame, the FX Matt Brewing Company.

CONSIDERATIONS: We recommend you call ahead, set times, and check for possible fees with the lockkeeper. There is no swimming. You may share the waterway with much, much larger boats. Restaurant names change, so don't look for Kitty's.

IS IT WORTH THE TRIP? For the lock experience alone, yes, it's worth it. The paddle itself can lapse into the routine, but it is a good outing, an interesting change, a different pace and pattern to a day on the water.

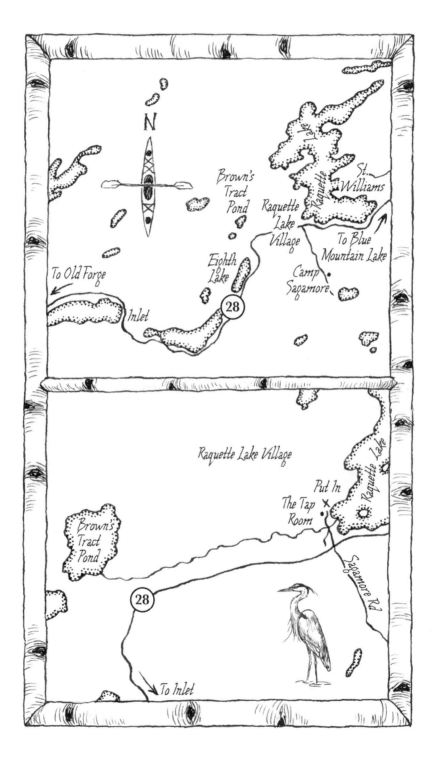

"Raquette City" to Brown's Tract Pond

This is a glorious day; rare this summer. Not on our scheduled Thursday, just a time when five of us have a free day. Also rare this summer. Heidi has warned us that this could be a challenging paddle, so we discuss our options. The decision comes down to whether we want to portage or paddle. The portage is short and the put-in is upstream halfway between Raquette and Browns Tract Pond, but we have all wistfully imagined ourselves on this course whenever any of us has crossed the bridge to Raquette Lake Village. We paddle.

THE WAY THERE: Take Route 28 north past Inlet and Eighth Lake State Park. There is a large wooden sign at the left turn to Raquette Lake Village. Cross the bridge and park in town. There is a public launch.

REFLECTIONS ON THE WATER: Putting in is easy. We unload our boats at the ramp in front of the general store and move our cars. There is a college student under a tent at the ramp informing the public (us) about two invasive species – Eurasian Millfoil and Zebra Mussels. He has written information and props to get his point across. We chat awhile, then, butts in boats, head out for today's adventure.

The water has been very high this year on all the waterways we have paddled, including this one, so we are able to pass under the bridge with no difficulty. We wander slowly upstream, crossing five beaver dams without having to exit our boats. Early on, we come to a bend where we spot a deer lying in the grass. He is a four pointer and in velvet. The youngster stands and watches us. We stare back. There is no movement save Audrey's hands tweaking the settings on her camera.

It is a long, leisurely paddle upstream in the warm, late-summer sun. We paddle on to a low bridge that Heidi says you can pass under. Carol, Ruth, and Audrey do. I am not a fan of spiders, so Artie and I drag our boats out of the water, up the bank, and across the bridge, and put back in on the other side. The muck on this side of the bridge is thick, black, and odiferous. We paddle

We have an audience

only about eight feet when we all have to sidle our kayaks up to a downed log. We get back out of our kayaks, balance on the same log, pull the boats out of the water, push them across and along the log, lower them into the water, and maneuver ourselves back into the cockpit. And we all do it without stepping in or falling into that disgusting sludge.

After a few more turns in the outlet, we arrive at Brown's Tract Pond. We have to cross over another bridge at this point, but we now have a small pond to explore where motors are prohibited. In the middle of the pond is a rocky island with a ladder where teens are jumping from a huge boulder. I fondly recall my daughter and her friends spending many an hour doing the same. There is a wonderful state park here that doesn't have even one bad campsite, though most are better for tents than trailers or RVs.

We paddle across the lake, agree we're all starving, find a rock, pull out, and have our lunch and a cold swim before exploring the

In the shadow of monoliths

rest of the pond.

On our return, we dread but again successfully conquer that log blocking the stream. As I pull my kayak across the bridge, a man and his son are entering their canoe. They inform us that we have passed a place where we could have pulled out at the shore and avoided the logs, the muck, the smell, and the bridge. Now we find out!

Once we are heading back to Raquette, we spot a heron that is trying to evade us. She flies ahead of us for a few yards, waits, and as we near, takes off again, lights, and waits. This happens five or six times. We all start laughing, wishing we could tell her that all she needs to do is fly behind our boats to avoid us.

The stream is bordered with clumps of pitcher plants, and I edge my kayak to peer in one. I get to thinking: in the past I have brought along camera, Peterson's guides for plants and birds, and binoculars, believing that I should be gleaning more knowledge from our forays. Today I admit to myself that I get my pleasure from simply soaking up the sensory environment. I savor the warmth of the sun on my shoulders and the cool of the water on my fingertips, the sound of the birds and the reeds blowing in the breeze, the sweet smell of the wildflowers and the foul stench of the mud, the beauty of the clear-blue, end-of-the-summer sky. I don't want to miss the flora and fauna because I am trying to read about, capture, and save the image. Today, I accept that all I want from the experience is the experience. Today I have grown.

I know that we are near the end of the paddle. I see the white steeple of St. William's Church in the distance. Just a few more turns downstream and under the bridge, and this glorious paddle is coming, sadly, to an end. I will treat to today's ice cream.

Silent sentinel

DIVERSIONS: There are hikes, Great Camp Sagamore, SS Durant, and other wonderful southwestern Adirondack diversions. For culture, most communities have music performances throughout the summer. A schedule is available in the Old Forge Visitor Center.

CONSIDERATIONS: If the water is low, you may be in and out of the boat several times between beaver dams and bridges.

IS IT WORTH THE TRIP? By all means. The Raquette Lake Supply Company is interesting. The Tap Room behind it is fun. There are three state campsites in the area – Browns Tract Pond on Uncas Road, Eighth Lake a few miles outside Inlet, and Golden Beach on Raquette Lake.

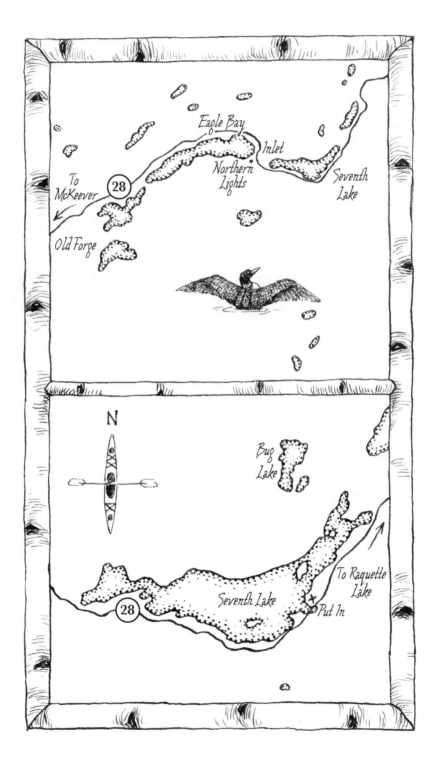

Seventh Lake

THE WAY THERE: Route 28 north takes you to Old Forge, through Eagle Bay and Inlet, and on. Seventh Lake appears like a jewel on the northern edge between Inlet and Raquette Lake. The public access boat launch is reached directly from Route 28. Don't be tricked into following signs for the village; the views from the bridge are lovely, but you cannot launch your kayak from the northern shore unless you have permission from one of the landowners. There are toilet facilities in the parking lot at the boat launch.

REFLECTIONS ON THE WATER: The number seven means luck in many cultures. The significance of the number goes beyond the obvious: seven seas, seven continents, seven colors of the rainbow; and the mundane: triple seven on the slot machine, being dealt or shooting lucky sevens in blackjack or craps. The nearby Oneida Indians believe that the tribe's rescue and rejuvenation will arise with their seventh sons. There are seven yogic chakras, seven Muslim heavens, seven Egyptian gods, seven Buddhist reincarnations. Pythagoreans find seven to be the perfect number: three plus four, the triangle and the square, the two perfect figures.

Unloading our kayaks in the parking lot of Seventh Lake, we

are inclined to agree. The morning is cool, threatens rain, but we do not care. We make introductions, reacquaint ourselves with fellow paddlers who've been absent this season until now, and eleven women set off.

We steer toward the north shore. The lake is smooth, the paddling easy. We've come further in the car than usual, and it feels good to be on the water of a Thursday morning. When our armada of colorful boats reaches the bridge that crosses the trail to Bug Lake and marks the easternmost limit to our paddle, we pause. We are a people of pausings, and today will bring us more cause to pause than usual. Listening for the sounds of the woods, we hear, instead, the sound of an approaching jogger. We grin at each other. Why not, we wonder? Everyone deserves a hand, a celebration. We park our boats in a row. Wait. When he bursts from the trees, we burst into applause. He runs on with a smile, and, I suppose, at least a momentary rush of adrenalin to make

Invasive species

his morning exercise better. Perhaps he'll remember us, this day: *...and when I came to the bridge, there were a bevy of women in boats, clapping and cheering for me from the lake. It was amazing.*

The weather has turned misty, and a fine rain falls. We tuck ourselves into slickers, under hoods, which mute the surroundings, make us more a part of the scene than simply spectators. The lake dwellers don't mind the rain, either. We spy a heron, a fishing loon. Our foremost find, though, is the exposed base of an overturned tree, a natural cathedral of intricately laced roots, tendrils woven of wonder and the search for water. We linger under its protection, its mammoth reminder that right side up and normal is not the only place to find beauty.

Then, as we reach a wider section of water and raise our heads into the raindrops, we happen on a boat. Not another kayak. Not a canoe. Not any craft we would imagine seeing here. A pontoon boat, from which divers in scuba gear plummet, around which buoys with red flags and other scientific paraphernalia float.

WOW women do what WOW women do. We investigate. We meet the captain of this DEC vessel and learn that he and his crew have worked their way north along the Fulton Chain this summer. Kathy asks a Kathy question. The swimmers submerge and begin their job of harvesting the invasive Eurasian Milfoil with a giant vacuuming apparatus. From the luxury of our boats, legs draped across their bows, we lean back and watch. We learn something every day. More on the days we let ourselves drift.

We lunch on a log in a line with our feet in the water near one of Seventh Lake's islands. We pass cherries and cheese, talk of families and absent friends. How our summers are going. (Our summers are going, that is a sad fact. Soon these Thursday adventures will be lost to work or weather. We cherish this one, this time, this lunch, this exertion, every moment.)

Today's group is big, and after lunch it splinters off into faster and slower segments. Though our westward travel meets with calm waters, we can see that the return trip is likely to be rough. Wind and waves have arisen. The lake is broad. One batch of us, the brave and hardy of the day, head on to the inlet at the west end. Others have already turned back. We linger, loath to give up any of what's left, then turn our boats to the wide waters and work our way up and across to the put-in.

It is a memorable excursion because we have reconnected with women from our first summer paddling. And nothing can be nicer than old friends. It is an exciting day because these are new waters for us. It is a perfect day, as every day in a boat on quiet waters tends to be, because despite the rain, despite a bit of roughness, we have escaped to a world we love. We don't need numbers to know how lucky we are.

DIVERSIONS: The primary rule for WOW women is this: there are no rules. That said, it should be noted that we consider it a crime against humanity to pass through Inlet without ingesting some homemade gelato from the Northern Lights ice cream shop. So we stop, sample, and savor.

CONSIDERATIONS: You may need an earlier start, depending on where you are coming from. The drive is long, but lovely.

Is it worth the trip? Isn't it always?

Lunch on a log

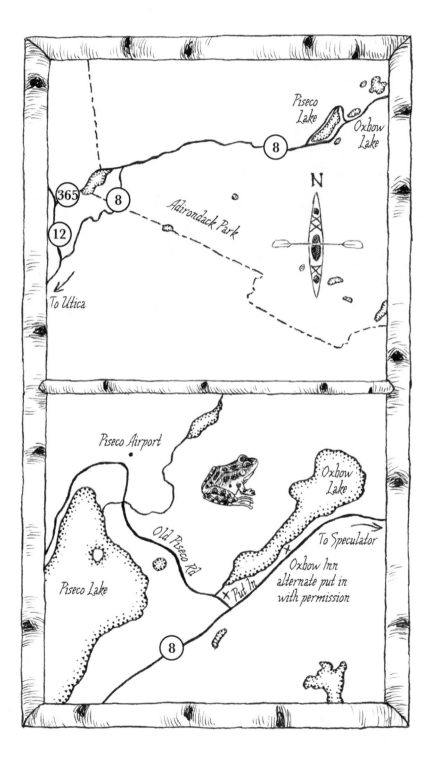

Oxbow Lake

It is gray and cold. I get a phone call from Carol.

"Are we going to do it?" she says.

"I am!" I reply.

"Meet you there."

It is settled.

THE WAY THERE: Take Route 365 east to Route 8. Turn left and continue to the Oxbow Inn on the left. The other option is to take the north end of Old Piseco Road and put-in at the bridge.

REFLECTIONS ON THE WATER: Bonnie and I are the last to pull in to the parking lot of the Oxbow Inn. Robin greets us and tells us that the owner has just come downstairs and is generously allowing us to park there. We unload and help each other carry kayaks across the lawn and down the dock. We slip our behinds into our boats and off we go. Thirteen of us this morning, and this is how we are connected: Heidi, Artie, Barb, and I all went to the same school, graduating within eight years of each other. Artie graduated with my sister and married Heidi's brother. Artie, Barb, and I lived on the same street. Barb and I lived next door to each other when our kids were in school. Carol married one of my best friends from high school. Carol, Barb, Ruth, and I were in a book club together. Bonnie was the superintendent who hired Ruth. Carol and Audrey taught together years ago. Pat drove bus when Bonnie was superintendent. Bonnie and Robin took an art class together. Artie brought Robin and Lisa, who moved here with her husband to farm. Artie's husband has been milking for Lisa (who also grows pumpkins). Pat went to school with my sister-in-law. Heidi brought Cathy who sings in a bluegrass band and went to school with my husband. Sue hooked up with us in earlier years; she is still working, so we don't see her enough.

It is a cold day. We are all wearing jackets. We find pleasure in the paddle despite the temperature and gloomy sky. The south side of the lake along Route 8 is lined with camps and homes, and we become voyeurs, comparing siding, windows, colors, styles, roofs, and docks. As we move along, the buildings thin out, and as we make our turn to the back side of the lake there are no more dwellings. We are on the wild side. Though it is windy, if we stay close to shore, we don't need to work as hard.

Barb was my hero when she was in middle school and I was in elementary. She taught me how to snap gum, smoke, dance the stroll, and ride a horse bareback. *This is how you do it. Get a boost up. Grab the horse around the neck. Friend slaps the horse's flank. Hang on for dear life.* I taught her not to accept gum from kids when she was a playground instructor – it may be a laxative!

She and I are chatting about our girls (now in their late thirties) and grandkids when we notice a rope swing hanging from a tree. I look at her, she looks at me. We both look at the terrain. The tree is at the top of a rock face sheer to the water. On the side of the boulder, there is an angled ledge to scramble up to the tree. There is a small area to pull our kayaks from the water, but it will be difficult to get out as there is neither beach nor shallow water, just the drop off. I push my paddle straight into the water to check the depth and can't feel the bottom. Again, we exchange looks in a silent dare. We both want the challenge and know if the temperature were twenty degrees warmer or we were twenty years younger, there would be no question. As it is, sadly, we don't rise to the occasion.

The weather has improved and the sun is out. We all paddle to the inlet which is absolutely jammed with water lilies. An occasional fish jumps, and more than once a frog hops from the lily pads into the water as we pass by.

Is thirteen an unlucky number? When we reach the end of the lake at the bridge on the road to Piseco, Audrey and Sue, who parked there instead of with the rest of us, are standing by their cars. Sue has locked her keys (and her cell phone) in her vehicle. Audrey has her phone but service in the area is not reliable.

Our offers to help are politely declined, so we paddle back to the Oxbow Inn for a late lunch and a glass of wine on the deck. Conversation is lively, with occasional musings about the fate of Sue and Audrey. Only later do we find out they eventually walked to the store on the corner of Piseco Road and Route 8 to call AAA.

DIVERSIONS: Speculator is a great little town with a good public beach, a fun department store, and a cemetery where French Louie is buried.

CONSIDERATIONS: Many areas that we kayak don't have cell service. Hook your keys to your bathing suit strap.

IS IT WORTH THE TRIP? It is. I want to go back on a nice day so I can try out that rope swing.

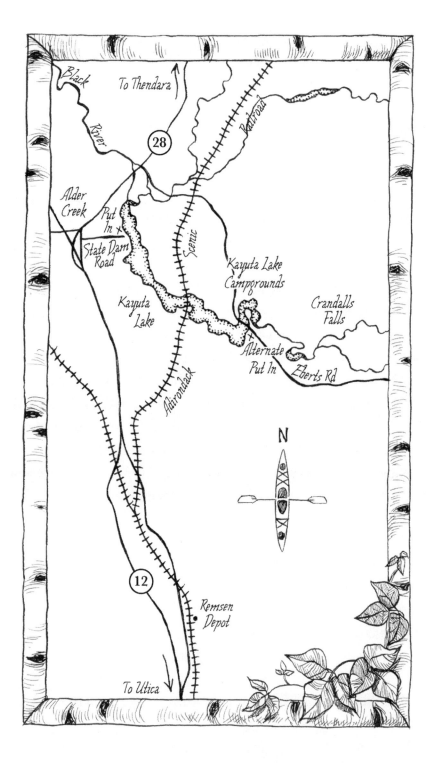

Black River

To Thendara

28

Railroad

Alder
Creek

Put
In +

State Dam
Road

Scenic

Kayuta Lake
Campgrounds

Crandalls
Falls

Kayuta
Lake

Alternate
Put In +

Eberts Rd

Adirondack

N

12

Remsen
Depot

To Utica

Crandall's Falls

Up a lazy river on a hot summer day is the best kind of paddling. That's when you pack a picnic lunch and point your boat toward Crandall's Falls. The trip is effortless, at least until you approach the falls, where the current picks up force and deboating can be interesting.

THE WAY THERE: Take Route 12 north to Alder Creek. Bear right on Route 28 and take a right on State Dam Road. There is a public launch at the end of the road.

You can access the Black River from many other points, including Ebert's Bridge, or, for a fee, the Kayuta Campground. We have made many trips from the various sites, but one of our more spectacular ones involved towing six kayaks of every color across Kayuta Lake with a rowboat and a seven horsepower engine.

REFLECTIONS ON THE WATER: The trip really begins as you leave the motorized bustle of the lake and pass under Ebert's Bridge at the northern end, entering a quieter world with many seasonal and year-round homes high on the banks of the river. Water lilies, pickerel weed, and other aquatic plants provide an impressionistic

Bringing them home

landscape with dragon and damselflies flitting on and ahead of our paddles. The river curves and eddies and soon begins to narrow down to a winding, twisting stream that promises a surprise with each bend...now a mossy log covered with basking turtles, next a great blue heron waiting for dinner to present itself.

There are few cottages along the stream, and one envies the inhabitants who choose to live in this peaceful environment. Humans aren't the only species that enjoy the area, however.

A discriminatory beaver chooses the banks of the river to form his hut, thus the name "bank beaver." The tangled mass of tree trunks and branches looks very much like the typical midstream beaver dam, but this is a residential structure, built into the mud along the riverbank.

Ducks and geese make this calm tract their seasonal home, a perfect place for hatching and raising chicks. They cruise along the shoreline looking for bugs, minnows, and other dinner items, not minding us as we invade their space.

After navigating a myriad of loops and turns, we begin to hear the rushing waters coming over the gently sloped falls. We find a rock or branch to secure our boats, climb the bank, and begin a short hike through the forest to a rocky outcropping where we can lunch, sunbathe, and splash in the clear, cold waters. (This path can offer challenges. Be on the lookout for poison ivy, and be prepared to slog through muddy areas after rainy periods.)

Occasionally, there will be others there, floating downstream and enjoying a respite from the outside world, having found a way to drive in, get a brief swim and picnic, and get back to their workaday schedule.

WOW girls, however, can laze as long as we care to, before returning on the same peaceful path. Life is good!

DIVERSIONS: Many good restaurants dot the country landscape nearby. The Adirondack Scenic Railroad trips that originate in Utica stop at the Remsen Depot, so there is opportunity to ride the train from there to Thendara and back, and they can accommodate bikes and kayaks if you want to take one along.

CONSIDERATIONS: You will want to wear long pants and foot cover for the hike, as poison ivy grows on the path to the falls. Also be aware of high water on the river, which creates cross streams at many places nearer to the falls. I found myself hiking in water up to my knees after a recent deluge.

IS IT WORTH THE TRIP? Repeatedly. The autumn is especially beautiful, with the leaves in full color – but, of course, every area that we frequent can boast of the same spectacle in October.

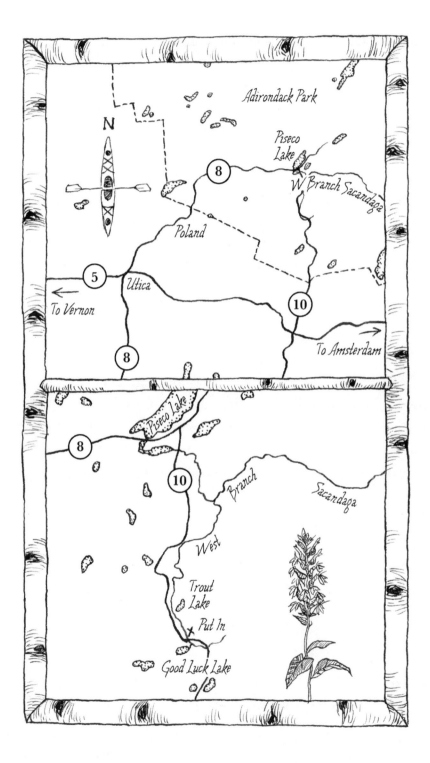

West Branch of the Sacandaga

All the wildflowers are gone. After an hour of paddling the river, that is what I notice. To be sure: it is the last Thursday in August.

THE WAY THERE: Take Route 5 east from Utica or Route 8 north from Utica until you reach Route 10. Take Route 10 north from Route 5 or south from Route 8. The put-in is approximately six miles south of Piseco Lake at the bridge.

REFLECTIONS ON THE WATER: Bonnie and I get a late start because when I pull into her driveway, we notice the smell of gasoline emanating from my ten-year-old pickup. This necessitates transferring the kayaks to Bon's car, one on top and one jammed up between the front seats and out the back end. Tie them both down with straps and bungees, go to gas up, and we are on our way.

Once we arrive, we pull off the pavement to park. There are men working on the bridge. We fear our trip will be noisy, not what we look forward to any week, but especially not on the last scheduled adventure of the summer.

Two women, one kayak down the bank; back up, repeat, until all nine of us have our boats in the water and our fannies securely seated in the cockpits ready to paddle downstream (which is due north on this part of the river). The sun is warm. The sky is the cloudless blue of fall. We are looking for Trout Lake, but the weeds and beaver dams have choked off the route. After crossing our third dam and our scout telling us we may as well retreat, we retrace our wakes and paddle upstream until we reach the bridge. The workers wave us through, and on we go to the outlet of Good Luck Lake. Jude leads. A beaver dam is blocking our access. Is this the way to spend our day? We decide to keep going on and see where it takes us. Paddling upstream presents no problems, and we leisurely snake up the river past banks and beaches looking for the best place for lunch. As the current picks up, we meet a couple who paddled down from another crossing on Route 10. We chat a bit, small talk. "Have you been here before?" "How far to the next bridge?" "Isn't it a gorgeous day?" And on we go. Meadows meet forest, and we all admire the way the sun dapples light on the ferns. We go on until it is clear that we will have to cross logs and drag kayaks along the river rock through the shallow current if we want to continue. We don't.

As we are paddling back to our beach of choice, it is then I notice. No flowers. Only shades of brown, green, and rust. The faded blooms and dried up pods ready to set seed for next year's glory.

We disembark on the sand to share our sandwiches and stories and ideas for next year's forays. It seems to me that we are all a little subdued, not our usual spirited selves. The teachers are going back to work next week. We all have obligations, plans for the fall – part-time jobs, babysitting grandchildren, new births. Let's just savor today.

Back in our boats, we decide to give Good Luck another try.

Sure enough; with a little more effort, Jude makes her way across the small beaver dam. As each of us passes, we pull a stick, eventually compromising the structure of the dam and easing the way for the paddlers to follow. What is left for us is just an easy glide through the slow water into the lake.

There is a man sitting by a campfire over on the south shore and a loon in the middle of the lake. Bonnie is, as usual, taking pictures with her new camera. Jude is reclining in her kayak, eyes closed, sleeping. I can't figure out how she does that. The rest of us are engaged in conversation or simply absorbing the scene with all our senses. We hug the north shore for awhile, examining the terrain for the perfect campsite. Another plan for next summer.

Artie, Heidi, and entourage head back to their cars. Now there are five of us, the original gals who started paddling together so many years ago, enjoying our collective solitude, one here, two there. Jude napping, Bonnie snapping, Ruth and Carol yapping. We are in no hurry to get around the lake. Then I notice. Two spikes of cardinal flowers...and some bottle gentian. Summer is not over. We still have weeks left. We can go together after the teachers get out of work. The rest of us can still go during the day. We vow to call each other, plan for next time. But as we paddle slowly through the outlet, in my heart I know real life will sadly encroach on our play days, and we will not be gathering en masse in our multicolored craft again this year.

Carol and Ruth's daughters have joined us at times; Bonnie, Jude, and I all have girls who have families and live away. I know they don't understand how much these weekly adventures feed our souls. And if they never get it, you can just bet that we are whispering it to our granddaughters so that maybe they can one day become just a few old girls on boats.

Noontime nap

DIVERSIONS: There are many other bodies of water in the immediate area.

CONSIDERATIONS: There are several access points to the West Branch of the Sacandaga along Route 10. Some are not suitable for launching a kayak. The last gas on Route 8 is in Poland. If you come from Route 5 there are more options.

IS IT WORTH THE TRIP? Definitely. Good Luck Lake feels much more remote than it is. And that is always a good thing.

Haps and Mishaps

Over the years, some of our aquatic faux pas have provided unintentional entertainment for the group, as well as those unfortunate onlookers who happened along. We begin to think of ourselves as "experts" when, in fact, we've never had professional instruction, and each new vessel or environmental variation produces challenges for which we are usually unprepared.

Example: After paddling in a "beginner's bathtub" for several seasons, I jauntily set out in my sleek new touring kayak with a confidence beyond reality. Having taken the camera and binoculars out of the drybag (in case the occasional eagle were to appear) and forgetting about them as the hours passed, I ever so sprightly attempt to disembark on a rock in the fast flowing current near Crandall's Falls. Needless to say, this wonderfully efficient boat requires agility beyond my custom and is soon floating upside down beside the empty drybag, as I flail about with waterlogged camera and binoculars around my neck.

Paddling the rapids of the West Canada Creek brings a totally new and exciting dimension to our experience. We have become accustomed to floating lazily down a stream or kicking our feet up (literally, on the kayak decks), and calmly soaking in rays on a hot

photo by Bonnie Sanderson

A surprise encounter

summer day. NOT on the West Canada. We struggle, we lurch, we're pitched fore and aft on the rocks, we practically collide with a surprised Holstein in the midst of her afternoon bath. There are many bruises on boats and bodies following this trip, but the adrenalin rush provides a rare excitement that we can't wait to replicate.

The mid-paddle swims in icy Adirondack waters; the encounters with critters, ducks, loons; the water ballet; sharing our stories, songs, and sorrows with others who really care; the "fun" of getting stuck in mud with kayak-loaded SUV's and pulling together to get out...memories of these and other WOW events keep us counting the days until we can throw off the winter blahs and pick up our paddles again.

What to Bring

DO BRING:

- Your U.S. Coast Guard approved Type III PFD
- An extra paddle for the group
- A bailer and sponge
- Rope and bungee cords
- A first aid kit
- Water shoes (for hiking and walking on rocky water bottoms)
- An inexpensive plastic poncho
- A whistle
- Enough food and drink for the duration of the trip

DO NOT BRING (OR WEAR):

- Jeans or cotton clothing
- Anything outside of your drybag, unless it's waterproof
- Cameras, binoculars, cell phones (except in waterproof bags)
- Expensive clothing, shoes, jewelry (they're irrelevant)

So much water, so little summer

Afterword

Some places you keep secret. A couple summers ago Carol and I stumbled on just such an Eden-spot. Miles down a bumpy stone road — our longest carry to a put-in we weren't sure was public — to the lake, a coin of copper-burnished brilliance in the woods. Just lying there, like any lost penny.

We boarded our boats, pushed off; we knew from the start we were blessed.

It was a day too big to fit into twenty-four hours.

It was the forest primeval at the lapping shoreline.

It was loons to the right of us and loons to the left of us, loon mothers with loon babies on their backs, stereophonic loon calls until we were lunatic with loons.

It was the easy glide of a small boat over dark waters reflecting a whole world, and the tired-muscle relaxation of paddling into the wind on our return trip.

And it was the indescribable thrill of rounding a tree-lined bend at the end of the lake, only to find more lake, at least another of this lake's length stretching out before us, promising an equal measure of pleasure on another day. The lure of a wild that won't wither.

So we won't name this lake for you, provide you directions, but instead, encourage you to find it, or its sisters, on your own. Strap your boats to your cars, toss in your life jackets and your paddles. Bring along a lunch, a bottle of drinking water. And awe.

Carry in your heart and head and hands the almighty awe for the world in which we walk. Let yourself smile as sunshine swallows your sorrows and wonder replaces your worries. Disembark and venture down any foot trail to the river, the creek, the rapids, the still pools where the answers are. Simply float on quiet waters until you are fulfilled.

The Adirondack environmental pledge of every outdoorswoman is "if you carry it in, carry it out." And so we dutifully pack up our granola bar wrappers and our sandwich bags, our tissues and any stray garbage left behind by other travelers, even our toilet paper. We "leave only footprints" and the memory of our paddle dippings, keeping the places pristine for the next passersby.

But what the brochures and books don't tell you is that though you leave no trace of your presence in the woods or on the waters, they will leave plenty of evidence of their existence in you. Every sojourn on still waters leaves you a little bit different, a little bit better, newer and knowing.

Join us. We're "just a few old girls on boats." It might not look as though we are working to achieve world peace on our weekly paddles. But we are. One boat at a time. On any mystery lake. If we meet you on the water, we'll share our melted chocolates and laughter, letting the vibrations of joy jettison to a wanting world.

The ballet

Perfect in pink

photo by Jude Dawes

Ode to May

by Jude Dawes

It is a flawless launch
balance and anticipation camouflage the reality
of sixty-six years, my hands smile as they grip the paddle
and we savor each slice of the blue beneath

Every word not spoken
is heard

I imagine an oversize wall clock, draped
and melting over the bow of my kayak, oddly reminiscent
of a famous Dali painting, drops of time fading
into ever widening circles of silence

The call of the loon
is humbling

From above, our aging flotilla might appear
a scattering of colorful, fragile, fall leaves
randomly floating, changing direction, dependent
on the wind and the prevailing current

Look again
a little closer

We *are* the prevailing current. colorful?
without a doubt...randomly floating?
often...changing direction? absolutely
fragile?

An unsuppressed chuckle
escapes

Startled, my new granddaughter May, flinches
big blue eyes thrown wide
"I'm waiting for you" I whisper, almost inaudibly
into the future that surrounds her

She drifts back to her peaceful place
and I to mine